A WOMEN IN HORROR POETRY COLLECTION, VOLUME 1

Under her Skin

EDITED BY LINDY RYAN & TONI MILLER

ISBN print: 978-1-64548-044-0
ISBN ebook: 978-1-64548-031-0

Cover Design and Interior Formatting by Qamber Designs and Media
Cover art © by Lynne Hansen
www.LynneHansenArt.com

Published by Black Spot Books,
An imprint of Vesuvian Media Group

This is a work of fiction. All characters and events portrayed in this novel are fictitious and are products of the author's imagination and any resemblance to actual events, or locales or persons, living or dead are entirely coincidental.

"It is women who love horror. Gloat over it. Feed on it. Are nourished by it. Shudder and cling and cry out—and come back for more." – Bela Lugosi

Table of Contents

FOREWORD *by Linda D. Addison*

Did you know *anthropodermic bibliopegy* is the practice of binding books in human skin? This is not a fictional concept from a horror novel—it's real! Look it up, but that isn't what this book is—no one's skin was used to make the cover, no actual blood used to letter the words.

This book of poems and prose poetry was written by women (cis and trans) and non-binary femmes under the theme of body horror. There are many ways to interpret this area and lucky for us, the work in this book covers a wide range from suggestive to explicit. Each poet has ripped away the skin of their soul's yearning to uncover hidden/suppressed emotions and wounds.

In spite of living in the 21st Century, the unspoken rules of society still haunt us. Skin: the lighter and tighter, the better; forcing an idea of body on us, that truly is horror. The impact of this unattainable physical perfection is revealed in several poems. Some show the relentless reshaping done by surgeons, slicing away again and again, to search for the impossible. Other poems reflect many ways the madness of the pursuit inspires cycles of self-mutilation with unapproved sharp items. We totter on high heels, covered in layers of makeup, while planning the next surgery to remove some here, place some there, and reshape ourselves in the image of a fallen angel, leaving only eyes unchanged to witness the insane results. Body horror or sad reality?

Some poems sing in dark fantasy of transformation to beings that speak like humans, but are they, or are they nightmares remembered so clearly they become real? Even the normal ability to carry life is either destroyed by the removal of the unacceptable or spun out of control with unimaginable multiple fertilization.

Other pieces put us in the arms of abusive lovers, diseased relationships with others and Self, where everything is surrendered, until nothing remains. There is verse where the expectations of others is regurgitated as uninvited bone structure in a body. Some work give the gift of recognizing the monster without, and waiting within. There are tales of being remade by ancestors and earth, of pain transforming into rage, and making abuse a two-sided sword bringing release.

Some are gentle pieces that flow classically and others are tough ones that vomit truth, each peels away the false veneer to show the meat and bones underneath that we disguise, so we can survive in a society that will eventually declare us too *old*. There is some freedom possible at that point, and strength.

Like a diamond with many facets, each poem/prose is another window under the skin of being/unbecoming Her. My shadow loved all of this, the true beauty beneath the thin, overworked outer layer of ectodermal tissue, because in the end, we were never the Final Girl. We are the Witch, the Myth, the giver of Life, feared.

—Linda D. Addison, award-winning author,
HWA Lifetime Achievement Award recipient and SFPA Grand Master

INTRODUCTION *by Toni Miller*

The collection you are holding is a true labor of love, born from a conversation between co-editor Lindy Ryan and myself about the resurgence of horror and the many amazing women writing horror poetry. Now, months later, an idea birthed between two women who love horror is making its way into people's hands—into yours.

As girls we are told horror stories dressed in the frilly, lace-trimmed guises of fairytales—woman trapped in castles, cursed into sleep and silence, preyed upon. As we blossom into young adulthood, we tell each other horror stories about girls who exhibit agency, identity, and are punished for it. As grown women we watch the news, rife with horror stories about how women's bodies are used and abused, considered property, treated as lesser-than. With these experiences in our hearts, it is no wonder we choose to explore their themes with our pens.

Women are held to social and beauty standards only attainable by altering our bodies or starving ourselves, body or soul. These everyday horrors surround us, demand us to reshape, to comply. Body horror speaks to women in very visceral and personal ways. It is no wonder, then, that we gravitate to body horror: the genre allows us to explore these terrors in a way we can control. In a way where we take our power back, allow our forms the freedom to truly be our own.

I was blown away by the number of submissions *Under Her Skin* received, and by the diversity and truth embedded within each line of prose. While the theme of body horror remains constant throughout this collection, topics range from motherhood to social discussions surrounding our bodies to a burning desire to retake control, to be *woman* within our skin. As a whole, this showcase illustrates through words and art how horrifying being a woman can be. How, at times, our bodies at times aren't our own, and how they can betray us in the most brutal of ways.

This collection is everything I love in body horror. I hope you enjoy it.

—Toni Miller, editor

NOTES FROM THE EDITORS

Lindy Ryan

Surely, there is no shortage of great poetry—and great poets—in horror today. Though the process of selecting which poems to include in this inaugural collection was, at times, a challenge, the difficulty was in choosing from amongst a pool of incredible submissions penned by both new and emerging voices of women and femmes in horror. In the end, this collection represents selecting those poems which best represented the collection's theme, and illustrated the diversity and intensity of women's voices in horror today.

Toni Miller

This was a truly difficult collection to edit. Each poem unraveled a bit of my soul while others tied it back up again. Some flayed my soul bare and dared to me to look in the mirror while others whispered in my ear while I slept. At the core of this collection is the everyday horror of being, of society, and of relationships. It has been an incredible honor to put this collection together.

Poems

HER
by Tabatha Wood

There's a hole in the world where the rot gets in,
engraved in blood and bone.
You placed your lips around it and sucked it dry.

Everything is broken now — meaningless and raw.
You lie, eyes wide, cracked lips pulled tight
like leaves of scrunched-up paper,
while snip-snap fingers weave your pain
with threads of sinewed silk.
Your memory maps are drawn in red,
connecting lines of gossamer,
as you spin your life with spider webs,
stitched criss-crossed on your wounds.

Your monstrous body opened, given freely, offered all,
now pummelled into silence by a myriad sliced demands.
In cold stripped rooms with side-stepped skins
choked black by the blood that you bore.
An aberration pushed, contracted, spewed out like soured bile.
Yet you mourn the destruction, the curse of lost time,
recalling the beast you once were.

Now you sway on the brink as you shriek at the sea
grief-choked and imbued with dark rage.
You crawl to your bed dismantled by loss
barren, a dull husk of yourself.
You howl at the skies and the vastness of space
hollowed out by the theft of your love.
And you reach to the lightness wrenched out of you,
voice cracked with your longing despair:

don't give me your sympathy, you beg, you plead,
don't give me your sorrow —
give Her back.

WE
by Morgan Sylvia

We're not what you wanted, are we?
We're not the perfect beings you designed
Our bones don't taste as you planned
And our dreams are dark and decadent
Far too gelatinous for your kind
I'm afraid we've strayed from the plan you so painstakingly wrought
You wanted velvet wings and compound eyes
Instead, we have leathery skin and pincers coated in keratin
We refuse the carrion you offer
And we only wake when the last light has bled from the sky
We know why you bound us and broke us and stitched us together
We've thought of these things, you know
Here in our shadows and our chains
But all is not lost, now, is it?
After all, we brought the things you asked for
The skulls filled with memories, the severed arms heavy with
violence
The bones full of pain
But it was never enough
Leave us
To our glorious midnights
Leave us to our rage
You never planned for this, did you?
You stitched us together from a hundred perfect corpses
But this isn't what you sought
You never thought that we would rise in defiance
You never thought we would rise at all
And yet here we are, standing before you in the thirteenth hour
Dressed in flesh and blood and bruises

Our torn striped stockings clinging to our battered legs
Turn your face to the moon, my mad creator
Before we claw your grizzled cheeks to shreds
Turn your shining eyes to the sun
Before we burn your sacred visions away
We never told you the price of our blood and our bones and our spleens
We never bargained the cost of our pain
Then again, you never really cared, did you?
You only wanted that moon-stained moment when feathers and claws burst through our skin
Let me ask you something
Did you ever factor the costs of your own parts?
Did you ever wonder how your liver would shine as we licked it?
How your congealing blood would run from our lips?
No, I thought not
We grow taller as you shrink before us
Your screams are out of tune, as were your dreams
We drink now the greasy arrogance that once rooted in your cerebellum
Your bones crack into slivers beneath our ivory fangs
We are your death, your deliverance, your reckoning
We are your darlings, your angels, your deliverance
We
Are your only saving grace

BEAUTIFUL
by L. Marie Wood

Beautiful.
Its tone, its texture, its interest: it's beautiful.
Eye-catching
eye-stilling
encapsulating
enrapturing.
Beautiful.
Fluid
under the skin, rippling
roiling
churning
like the waters of the sea
like the boiling in a pot
hand inside to unravel the skin
peel it
flay it to reveal
Blood
red, like
roses and lips and apples and…
Banksia
Wild and pure
Light inside
Cut, cut to see the beauty inside
arm, leg
hips where flesh curves to make them look.
Breast make them stare, keep them shook.
Hibiscus to heal what ails.
Blood let to purify
nullify

beautify.
Sure
Unsure
But still, so beautiful
Even as it spills
even as it dyes
even as it boils, never diluting, never dispersing
Never
Because it takes its rightful place
Always
Always
Red and bright and dark and bruised
Always
Beautiful, trumping all.
The glint of the knife catching the light and before the strained
edge
Stained edge
Blood red
Wet with blood… dense and red
And still
And always
Beautiful.

SKINCARE ROUTINE
by Cynthia Pelayo

First there is washing, followed by moisturizing
Soon defense from Ultraviolet rays, in levels
Sun protection factor indicated in numeric
Intensity, to penetrate and prevent burns, cancer
Aging, and what is aging, but wasting before the
Public, and so there are more creams, layered
Slathered, eye treatments for dark circles, puffiness
Products to apply to my neck to prevent the signs of
Dryness, sagging, spots. Maybe I need more collagen?
Should I exfoliate or add a serum? Although, what
Is a serum versus essence? I want to look fresher and
Younger, and why is my skin so delicate and thin?
Morning cleansers followed by liquid foundation
To fill in the cracks. Then I contour and blend and

Blush, shadows and liners, mascara and setting spray
To finish a look that now requires hyaluronic acid
Retinol, which fails to prevent the deepening and
Drooping. So, then I let them poke then prick with
Botulinum toxin. Some days we plump and fill with
Acid-based fillers, Juvéderm, but then the forehead
Frown, crow's feet, tear troughs, bunny lines,
Nasolabial folds, marionette lines, neck creases and
Crepe décolleté all return, and once again I must
Ten-step, twelve-step skincare, inject and fill, laser
Resurface, and wouldn't it all just be easier to stop
The stinging, the burning of all of these regimes
Carve and slice the outline of my face and peel it
Gently back, expose fat and blood and bone, and
Shiny cartilage. I'll allow you to mold and cast for me
At once an unmoving, unblinking eternal mask

MY SKIN
by Cindy O'Quinn

I need to go away from myself in order to heal. Be separate from my body, and the way skin makes me feel. Anesthesia licks my veins. Waking inside a nightmare as I tumble through space. External pain works its way inside, attached to my soul—kissing my face. That very pain becomes part of me like the color of my eyes. Those are the scars that weave their way in.

Stretchmarks of life...

Outside my mind. Threadbare like macramé. The scars unravel. Loosely woven, threads no longer tight. Cut it out. Let it go. One slice at a time. In dreams, life floats away. I can simply be. Change—it stays the same. All but the pain left on display for everyone to see. Chest flayed open. Exposing every part of me. Take me back before it all started. Before the pain.

...when skin was just skin. And not a home for my fucking scars.

ACCEPTABLE FEMME
by Tiffany Meuret

Epidermis:

Epi—Greek meaning for 'over' or 'upon'. This is the outer shell. The Stratum Corneum (Once thought to be biologically inactive. Not true. It is composed of terminally differentiated keratinocytes. Alive, in fact. What a wonder. They wait to be desquamated, or shed, like one would scrape scales from the corpse of a fish).

Remove the eyes covering the body (the scales). Eyes to watch and watch and watch. These only get in the way. Laser focus is required. Avoid too much sensory information, if possible. Scarring is inevitable, but it should heal. In time. Pain is part of the process.

Dermis:

Basement layer. Multiple subregions. Watch out for the reticular region, in particular. Venom sacs must be denatured. Despite popular myth, these sacs are potent. Feral. One drop can kill a grown adult in seconds. Dissect carefully. Infection risk is serious. Wounds are slow to heal, this cannot be avoided. Don't bother trying. The process is sufficient.

Subcutaneous Tissue:

Serrated teeth attach themselves to the muscles. Extraction must be meticulous. Incisors are sharp and plentiful. This is evolutionary. Marvelous. Recommend specimens be preserved

for further display and study.
Peak risk of subject death. Melt the fat while there. Couldn't hurt.
/Uh-oh!/ You got greedy, didn't you/Understandable/Not the
first, not the last/

The Inner Sanctum:

Old, like putrid gore. Too far *too far* TOO FAR. Stop. Shrapnel
warning. Cover your ears. Cover your ears and run. Run. You do
not belong here! You do not belong here.
Run.

INSIDE OF ME
by Betsy Nicchetta

I will never sleep again!
The kicking never stops!
I have not started counting
every single life inside of me….

Couldn't resist the boy's caresses,
pressing closer and closer to me
until he entered inside of me….

Fertilizing ever single egg in my body

Cursed at birth…

Every single egg inside of me
would fertilize all at once….

Doctors marvel over me
I'm some kind of medical marvel,
no woman as ever carried this many babies at once,
A world record lies inside of me

Night and day
numerous kicks inside my uterus
keep me constantly awake
And I wonder what lies inside of me….

CORPORATE KEYBOARD
by Betsy Nicchetta

Clickity, click, click, click….
Perpetually typing…

Click, clickity, click…
Stopped writing my own words years ago…

Click, clickity, click, click, click…
Cold metal attaches wrists to the desk…

Click, click, click, clickity…
Muscles are completely stiff…

Longing to stand to stretch my legs…
But I must continue...

Click, click, click, click….
On the keyboard fingers fiercely tap…

Click, click, clickity, clickity…
The corporate demon demands to type
every word ever said….

METAMORPHOSIS
by Caitlin Marceau

Crooked, off-centre, masculine.
That's how it started,
words burrowing like termites,
festering inside,
rotting the foundation,
until she corrects a problem
that had never been there.

Small, uneven, boyish.
The offhand comments men make,
measuring her womanhood
by judging her body,
commodified without consent,
implanting opinions and silicone
inside her.

Heavy, disgusting, enormous.
The thoughts they let her hear
through their long stares and small sizes,
making her unwelcome in public spaces
and hate herself in private ones
so much that she thanked them
when they carved out her stomach.

Soft, blemished, sagging.
The opinions shared by experts
pinching her skin, pulling it back,
as they disapprove of the happy memories
and laughter marking her face,
until the sting of the needles
numbs her to their criticism.

Dimpled, stretched, loose.
The magazines scream at her
covers waving perfect bodies
like bright red flags,
warning her of imperfections,
so she'd ask them to cut off the excess
and pull her flesh taut.

Plastic, fake, monstrous.
The words that come to mind
when she looks in the mirror
and finds her eyes,
the only things left unchanged,
and sees them in a face she doesn't recognize,
but everyone calls *beautiful*.

IT HURTS WHEN I BREATHE
by Mercedes M. Yardley

There's something growing inside
spores in my lungs
tendrils in my brain

Deadly oleander unfolds in my eyes,
nightshade burrowing in the diseased sockets
of my teeth

Every time you say,
hey woman

Or
server girl

Or
hey there, Las Vegas whore
when I'm holding the hands of my trembling children

Your words spread seed

At night, I scratch at my skin
a hand rake slipping obscenely
into the dirt
uninvited.

Vines and leaves poke
through
and it hurts. It always hurts.

I bite my rage back, swallow
it down, and the pits grow inside
like children.

I am Mother Earth, I am a
carrion corpse
giving rise to the broken reeds inside

I run the knife
under the skin of my arm
hemlock springs free
white snakeroot
Cut away the refuse
The weeds in the garden
The briars in the grass

Look, look, look,
I say

vomiting Belladonna and bloodflower

and my eyes are on stalks
erupting from my sockets like rosary peas

My lungs are veins and jungle rot tangled together.
It hurts when I breathe.

DESIGNER GIRLS
by Elsa M. Carruthers

Our flesh will be cut
into submission
If necessary.
(It's always necessary)

Custom-made cootchies
cinched up just as he likes

Spent uteruses are
predicted to spill,
so out with them; young med students

Need time with sutures
to make our seams look flat,
undetectable

And us girls with the fat noses
and lips, we'll pay double.
Sooner or later
we'll slink back for the "mommy make-over"

Go under scalpel to
slice and dice and
toss folds and fat
while breasts stretched with milk and age
are hoisted up, tacked into place

Lasers erase our motherhood, leaving
skin smooth and taut,
Like plastic or melted cheese

Areolas and anuses bleached pure.
Our faces and necks must match.
Tug and tug until
We look like plucked geese.

SANCTIFICATION
by Amanda Kirby

My eyes offended
I plucked them out
Fingers slipping underneath
Vessels and sinew snapped

My tongue cursed
In vain
I bit it through
Tasting iron on the jagged remnants

I loved the soothing scents of home
This is not my home
And so my nose went too

My fingers loved
The touch of myself
My feet the warmth of sand
By my breasts my brothers stumbled
I took the knife to all of them

All pleasures of the flesh discarded
Fingers, feet, breasts, and bud
And wrapped in bloody rags
Crawling towards you

Handless
Footless
Faceless
Nameless

Am I worthy now?

I CUT AWAY THE PARTS THAT OFFEND YOU
by Elsa M. Carruthers

The puckered silver of my stretch marks.
The ripple of stubborn fat between my thighs,
I scrubbed them off with the SOS pad a wire brush

Never mind the blood, it will scab over.

The heavy veins on my legs and feet are easier to get to than
the thin spidery ones that run from the tweezers and needle I
use to excise them,
but the effort has left me feeling breathless and lighter

One step closer to blemish free.

For my face, I don't know
Mellon baller could work for the bags under my eyes
And I suppose I could shave down that hook at the end of my nose
with a cheese grater. You tell me when to quit

Was there anything else?

SOMETHING THAT NEEDS DESTROYED
by Linda M. Crate

when you make your body
the villain
food becomes the enemy

there is no comfort
except when you're sleeping
because there you can escape
the nightmare of reality,

but you always wake up
having to face the music;

want to be anyone but you
and wonder how anyone could love a
body like this?
you loathe it,
but it doesn't go away simply with
your hate and your rage;

cannot exist without your body but instead
of loving it you think of it as a cage

something you always want to break out of
and something that you need to escape,
something that needs destroyed.

MAGNIFICENT
by Desiree Abalos

This blade,
filling the air with metallic ambiance.

Magnificent
this broken doll,
quiet, permitting further incision,

Paleness of skin shining.
I nick a finger as I am distracted by her neck,
pulsating in my mind, sweat beading,
salt

     over within seconds.

Magnificent
the way the body works, its function,
more enthralling when the lungs give out.

A macabre wish to examine,
a fancy.

SMILE
by Nico Bell

Smile,
She says.
"I can't. I'm dying."
Don't be dramatic,
She says.
She props the hospital pillows
so I straighten my back
and she reaches into her overnight bag
to pull out a tube of Angel Blush Pink lipstick.

Pucker,
She says.
And I try.
God, I try

because I want to give her
a moment of joy
but I'm so exhausted.
I don't have it in me to smile.
She frowns
as I shake my head
and she steps out of the room
mumbling about staying positive.
And I know she's ready
to call it quits
even though my body will soon
call it quits and I know
She deserves a smile before I go.

My gift
To Her.

I reach for her purse
and I pull out the small pocketknife
she carries for safety.
I begin to carve.
The blade slices at the corner of my lips
tearing apart the skin and tissue and veins and cells
a heat mixed with salt of tears and iron of blood burns,
as my lips expand,
as my teeth are exposed,
as my grin stretches from ear-to-ear.
She returns into the room
and sucks in a breath.
My, God. What have you done?
She asks.

"What you wanted."
Blood drips down my chin
as I
Smile.

UNBECOMING PORCELAIN
by Nikki R. Leigh

Mouth of cotton, screams trapped
Behind wads of flesh upon flesh
Echoing like mouths into mouths.

The undoing of skin
To hardness, encasing muscle, tendon
Stiff, joints arthritic laid bare
The doll you hold is me, now, the doll is me.

Painted thin, white, bright behind a wall of resin
Glassy eyes have long since squeezed real eyes away.
Legs hang, arms droop, backs arch, no control
Tattered dress, lace fringe.

The ground is unforgiving, shattering skin like dropped glassware
pieces scattering in every direction I feel some go out and some
go in and some are me, but most are you.

Skin seizes, webbed by glue hot between my pores
Becoming whole again
I wait to unbecome.

WHAT THE DEAD GIRL IS TRYING TO SAY THROUGH WHAT'S LEFT OF HER MOUTH
by Lindsay King-Miller

The secret is that it feels good to die
and yet not fall. To walk the world, awake,
decaying, singing joy with rotten tongue,
to hear the death throes of each mortal cell
chiming a note in the celestial scale.
To be captain, not captive, of this corpse.
My ragged body does not yearn for rest:
life was a lurid dream, and now I rise.
It hurts. I love the hurt. My broken teeth
scream symphonies as we devour the world.
All that I eat becomes me. My own heart
a trembling feast, the succulence of fear.
Come, suffer with me. Let me love your bones.
I bear this sweet infection in my kiss.

ANYTHING BUT WHAT IS
by Linda M. Crate

you look in the mirror
finding your body
the villain
unsightly and unseemly
it must be defeated

you don't rationalize
that you need your body
or that it could be beautiful as is,

you fail to see the true villain
is society;

you buy into the myth
that you're not good enough
and your body always needs to be
made better somehow—

it is disgusting, it is too large or too small,
too imperfect and too unworthy of love;

you want to cut it,
become invisible,
make your body anything
but what it is.

WITH BLOOD
by Jennifer Crow

Without blood, how do starfish know
when they are dying?
Fishermen tried to exterminate them, carved
meaning from the pebbled flesh of their arms
knives busy each time the lobster pots rose
dripping from the depths, saving bait
for the intended victim, but their efforts
yielded only more mindless enemies
in endless creeping arrays. You can't kill
a starfish by cutting, not without
extraordinary care, and meantime
the lobsters starve.

    Under my nails
blood taints the skin, the keratin. Still
I dig a little longer at the dry patch
along my spine, maybe etching a scar
I can't see without standing on tiptoe
before the mirror, neck craned,
examining each freckle and mole
for signs of imminent death.
Sometimes impulses lurk, predatory
and omnipresent, the itch
at once within reach
and insatiable. I rinse my fingers
under the tap and grimace
at my reflection. Even starfish know
how to reach into a trap
and find that morsel of bait.

HARM
by Emily Ruth Verona

I pulled
an incisor

from my arm,
bloody

at the
root.

That's how
I learned.

This hate
you bear

toward
yourself,

grows
teeth.

SNAKESKIN
by Stephanie M. Wytovich

With wet earth beneath my feet,
I drink the moon out of the sky,
feel the stars on my face, that familiar
tickle down my back. She calls to me,
the charmer, teasing me out of my skin,
her voice a summons, a silk-wrapped whisper

> I dance,
> I slither

My flesh sags, slides off my bones,
I am secrets and sundown, this shedding
a sacred act, my body a prayer, a sacrifice
to the scales. I slip into myself, collapse
surrender, the serpent's song screaming,
a hiss, a spell, the poison in my veins

> I slide
> I shake

This form is sanctuary, venom,
my blood a rattle, my pulse a viper's
bite. I am tongue-forked and coiled,
my eyes two opaque coins. Watch
for me in the grass, in the water. I am
nesting, I am resting, this shape a
a solitude, a safe haven until

> I stir
> I strike

EN ARE ALL ONE MONSTER

ra Windwalker

I am my father's daughter but my grandmother's heir:
my mother's brother has taught me
the ready wisdom of the magpie
and the patience of the bear – still, you found me
unready, unwoken, unwise,
and I did not see the wild dog in your eyes
until my own swam with brine
and you held me down, down, down
in the icy tide:
I called on my mother's guardians,
I became salmon, became seal, became seaweed
in your grip, but you held on through every shift:

with the last breath I stole from the sea,
I made snakes of my hair
and with my starving heart turned yours to stone:
you are not so special and strange
as you imagine, and my sisters and I
know your poor brood wherever you wander,
wherever you hide, by this echolocation of the soul
practiced by all the spirits of the wood,
the spirits of the muskeg,
the spirits of the mountains and the tundra and the sea.

you made me my brother's unfound,
but now you will find me everywhere:
mine are the hands that seize your ankle
from the forest floor, mine the mouth
that sucks you down in the mud,
mine the laughter that mocks your man-mimicry

in every gust of wind and burble of the river,
mine the heavy paws that pound
after you on dark tracks, mine the belly
that will one day grind all your bones,
make mess and mucous of all your muscle and your will.

you have not undone me,
but I am every day unwinding you,
unspooling you cell by cell.
I am the rocks you cannot crush
the concrete that will wall you in,
the pauper's stone that will mark your end.

I am my grandmother's heir.

WHEN THE WITCHES CAME OUT OF US
by Donna Lynch

We all remember
When we felt the witch wake up
But we may not remember why
And for the purpose of our preservation
We forget so much
We look the other way…
But not the witch

She tried to get out
The first time
Someone was where they shouldn't have been
The first time
The fifth time
Or every time
Someone told us to be quiet…
But the witch cannot stay silent

She tried to get out
When some of us started to bleed
And all of us started to change
And everyone else was trying to get in

And told us to open wide
And told us to close our eyes…
But the witch will never blink

She tried to get out
Every time our body was not ours
Every time something was inside us
That invaded, uninvited

In our heads
In our torsos and our hearts
Anywhere and everywhere
That could be entered
She tried to climb out of our mouths
Every time we screamed…
The witch was waiting

And if we never set her free
That choice is ours and ours alone
She will be still if we say so
For the purpose of our preservation
Stitch her away with her own red thread
Keep her inside with her very own curses
But someday
If we need her
She will do what she must to protect us
She will tear us back open to get out
And we will find that
all those ugly things we made ourselves forget…
The witch hasn't.

PROSERPINE
by Antonia Rachel Ward

i do not remember when
i swallowed the seed
only the sensation of it
sour and unsatisfying
slipping down my throat.

it lodged in my chest,
flowering tumorous
accumulations
beneath smooth skin,
beginning a slow rot.

you spectate
as i eat myself,
consuming my own
bilious sweetness,
product of aeons
of decay.

i am the underworld.
a sublime mistress,
source of fascination
and fear.

you might hold me—
at arm's length.

you might worship me—
from a distance.

but when I surface
in the springtime,
black with decay
vomiting feelings,
and crawling with putrefaction—

you will not let me near.

WINNOW
by Tiffany Michelle Brown

You have such a tiny waist
My lovers say.
Their hands explore my flesh,
Claim my skin,
And each one takes a piece of me with them
When they leave.

Every time, my midsection is left askew,
Unbalanced and undone,
Hollowed out by their desires.
I carve fresh notches into my belts
To keep up with the winnowing.

You're tiny,
So tiny, they gasp,
Delighted by my narrowness,
My nothingness.
Their words are cold against my skin,
But I want them to want me,
And so, they take and take and take.

And I let them
Until I can't anymore.

My current lover,
He stares at my waist and smiles,
But the shape of his mouth is wrong.
He grimaces when he sees my spine,
Knowing there is nothing left of me to claim.

MY TAINTED TOUCH
by Mary Rajotte

In the darkest confines of my mind
regret lurks like a feral beast.
When at last it awakens,
it scratches with talons
barbed and marrow-deep,
taunting me with
venomous
dread that
seeps
its
blight deep
into my
innermost core.
And like that of a
contagion, bitterness
contaminates my every
moment, sullies my every breath,
defiling you with my tainted touch.

UNTOUCHED
by Marilyn Fabiola

All I want is
skin you have never touched
a body, an existence
you never devastated

doused
scalding water
burnt flesh
scrubbed raw
never to be clean

you seeped into me
your parasitic presence
gnawing

urged to be torn apart
lifting abraded skin with a blade
severing from complicated ligaments
blood rivulets flow
coil down my legs

with each scrape
unveiling
more muscle
tendons and sinew
my old skin slips around my ankles limp and wet

exposed
red meat and viscera beneath
now I am
the only parts you never touched

feverish relief
I am sublime

NIGHTFALL
by Stephanie Athena Valente

in this memory, i am dead.
my body is on an altar. the ritual, complete.

stars hidden under my nails.
i am myth: breath, pain, longing.

i am the protagonist in a horror movie
a vision in white: always beautiful.

was i an ill-fated bride, or the babysitter,
carrying a demon inside her?

it doesn't matter because i am dead.
the moon pools blood and ripens like my belly.

i casted a spell because i wanted to live.
the demon brought me here.

yellow roses, white roses strewn along my body.

my dress is beautiful. i am not wearing shoes.
the moon shines big and bright.

i am sleeping forever. i want to sleep forever.
i want to bathe in blood.

instead, my muscles lurch. a hand, a wrist, flickering.
now a limb. electricity blood.

it feels like sex. it feels like vomiting everywhere.
i am not even sorry.

the moon howls, it haunts. i am born.
teeth so sharp. muscles so hard.

i eat the flowers. nectar is in the blood.
i am not quite human, not yet.

THE RIGHT FREQUENCY
by Jessica McHugh

My body erupts
in a riot
of ghostly roots
braving my heart
like a hunt
    skinned
    toothless
    mounted
I grow in sleep
    stretching
    doubling
    splitting
the dead remember
nothing but themselves
and veins that slip
like love notes
under your door

WORDS UNSPOKEN
by Mary Rajotte

I want to go
where darkness grows,
deep beneath the fetid earth.
I want to drown
in the endless night,
Beneath the weeds I'll lay
and wait for you.
No stars, no moon
shall touch my eyes.
No heat, no warmth
shall soothe my bones.
When at last I settle,
 when I wither and waste away,
  weeds shall thread through my skin,
  blossoms shall spring from my lips,
  and blooming, they shall whisper
  all those words unspoken.

TO BLOOM IN BLOOD
by Sara Tantlinger

It came from the garden
crept around the flowerbed
deposited a kaleidoscopic petal path
behind its twisted body
slithered between your pores
leaving a horrible prickling as it sank
beneath dirt-smeared skin

You rake nails against your arm
yet still the itch persists, insatiable
and burrowing beneath epidermis
until the feathery sting
blooms throughout your blood,
begging to be scratched away

Scrape garden shears
over and over and over
until skin peels back like flaying
rinds from fruit, exposing flesh
and then bone, from ulna to humerus
ribbons of muscle undone, and you tug
at sinew and veins, unwrapping yourself

Plow into crackling marrow
and scarlet-stained pus, slash blades
against your skeleton, listen to the song
of meat screaming as you murder yourself,
but the itch lives on, insatiable, slithering
its slick body up your arm, across your chest
depositing phantasmagoric petals

inside the aching acid of your gut

Plant your body between daffodils and lilacs
the deeper you sink into the flowerbed,
the less the itch persists, allows your body to cool,
allows your roots to cling and sprout here
until new owners arrive, rake into the dirt
sow something pretty and wild, but instead
you will bloom from the garden, slither inside
pores until they scratch and unstitch skin,
until they bleed every drop into your earth

SHREDDED ALTERATIONS
by Sara Tantlinger

change
never comes softly
never brushes your cheek
with butterfly wings
never leaves sparkling
dust behind on your nose

change
shreds its way inside
parting your skin
with barbed wire
sepia-toned rust marks
bleeding across bruised flesh

change
steals your breath
sends cotton to live inside
your heaving lungs,
dries your heart into a raisin
demanding you wait out
the pain until it allows
water, until it allows
freedom

change
comes fast now,
blink once, twice
water drowning out the cotton
reviving your pruned heart
like new blood come to swim

the canals of your sacred veins
come to remember your stories
of the past, of the present

awakening, reckoning

you cannot force the caterpillar
to change, you can
only wait, can only
nourish the body for so long
can only
hope nature wants your
transformation
to be beautiful for once

THE DEEPEST CUT
by Nancy Brewka-Clark

The belle of the ball, she lies partially gowned,
an unlikely debutante at the center of attention.
Like Queen Victoria she will succumb to oblivion
in a netherworld where birth pangs are banished.

An unwilling debutante at the center of attention,
she eyes the umbilicus of an IV drug given not for
the strength to bear infants as Victoria did nine times,
but an abdominal excision to extract cells gone rogue.

The plastic IV tube glistens like a stalactite of ice
as she, Regina Vagina, sinks into the numb embrace
of royal ether in a palace chamber white as snow,
having kissed off her ovaries, cervix & womb.

Having bidden adieu to ovaries, cervix & womb,
she drifts off on a gurney turned Victorian swan boat,
wanly supine beneath the blade of a masked pirate
surgically snatching damaged plunder, blood rubies.

She will awake not to a prince's kiss but a silent ring
of swathed minions peering down at her as she lies
on the gurney, macabre ball of a queen's dream gone,
her body hollowed, no raw life beginning anew.

STRANGE BEDFELLOWS
by Angela Sylvaine

I invite you into my bed
Savor your warmth pressed close
But dream of scuttling insects
Feathery hair caressing soft skin
    antennae that smell and taste

Awoken by the stab of pain
I lie alone in the dark
Fingernails find the rising weal
    scratch the mark you left
Or were you even real?

That pained spot spreads
Nibbling at my unmarred flesh
Pocks ooze with yellow venom
That wafts a carrion scent

The itch is my obsession
Scratching the only blessed relief
But then the fire burns hotter
Flaming until I'm charred and flaking

Something squirms within me
Born and biting from inside
My nails tear skin like paper
Welts become gaping wounds
    stung by salty tears

A sound escapes my throat
Laugh or cry or scream
Bloodletting is the way

And skin splits freely now
    toxins ride a river of red
With worms colored like clotted cream

Hollow now of my nightmare's children
    I sag and deflate
But they take part of me with them
As they seek a new host

SOFT BOX
by Amy Grech

Red
Wet
Blind
Writhing
Worm

Soft Box
Locked
Inside
Him
Rare
Parts

ELDRITCH MOTHER
by Melodie Bolt

Apega of the Void, skin automaton
bloated with otherworldly ruin,
her massive elm-arched abdomen
swimming with root rot and fetid matter,
reverberating with the glub of undulating fetus—
the Immortal Abomination of Abominations.
While cosmic horrors, predatory with expectation,
alien eyes squinting under Atlantic waves,
strain to discern the adumbrations
of Necronomicon lullabies.

OUTSIDE IN
by Dalena Storm

The mess crept up from the outside in
So she paid it no mind at first
She spotted dirt in the corner, then a zit on her chin—
A coincidence, surely, at worst.

Those were the days when the moods would strike
Like a bat caught her right in the chest
As the grime crept up and the gloom swept in
she retreated like a bird to nest.

There were pockets of sunlight, for a while, to sleep in
And counters free of mess,
And through the long hall she sashayed like a bride
Swishing dust from the hem of her dress.

Then one fine day when she opened her mouth
Out crawled first an ant, then a spider;
The bugs that she thought she'd swept under the rug
Had taken up residence inside her.

Her house was her home, and her home, her body
No difference between the twain
Now through all her veins is running the sludge
She had thought was confined to the drain.

She's coughing out roaches and sneezing out mold;
Her lungs can't expel all her sin
For the mess she had thought was outside her at first
has always been under her skin.

ZOMBIFICATION
by Roni Stinger

Filaments poke through my palms. I rub and wash,
flush them down the drain.

They return with others, sprout between fingers and toes.
Remove and rebound, again and again.

Strange thoughts fill my skull—find dark and moisture,
hide and be still, go to sleep. The orders move into my joints
and muscles, crystallize beneath my skin.

I've seen the ants sculpted into foreign bodies. Mandibles latched
into a tree. A breeding ground. Horned husks for fungus renewal.

Thank God it only happens to insects. Thank God I'm not a bug.
My microbiome speaks. My skin ripples, legs and arms move
of their own accord.

I crawl beneath the house, letting the Cordyceps grow.

MOLTING
by Roni Stinger

Skin turns thin and dry. Age spots, wrinkles,
and crow's feet for birthdays.

Moisturize and spackle. Sand and tuck.
Grasp youth until it tears. Clumps of wet
tissue cling to hands, reveal atrophied muscles,
degenerating bones. Cartilage floats.
Joints click and clack.

Skin sloughs and hangs, a gauzy membrane,
girdles can't contain. Wriggle and rub, forward
and out. Discard chimeric standards.

Sinews stretch, an exercise of metamorphosis.
Venom courses through tongue, spitting darts
to change the world.

INTIMATE COMMUNION
by Roni Stinger

I reach inside,
spill innards
at your feet.

Blood and bile
veil my tongue.
Pungent putrid offal.

We stare
at the goo
and grotesquerie.

Pick through pieces,
feeling for sustenance.
Hands thick with rot.

Emptied. A hush
before you. Cellophane
skin. Brittle bones.

You walk away,
my entrails stuck
to your shoe.

MIDNIGHT MAELSTROM
by Monique Snyman

A well of darkness, deep
deep down; poison leeches through
contaminating the inside.
Painful memories return, unavoidable
all-consuming; clawing at thin bone
meant to protect grey matter.
A trickle of destruction, drip
drip despondence; toxicity spreads
infecting the mind.
Problems intensify, overwhelm
defeat; forcing the seal open
until cracks form.
A deluge of emotions, dig
dig desperation; knife slices across
purifying the ache.

SYMBIOTIC BEASTS
by Marge Simon

Marlana comes to me with smiles,
a sign she's ready for coition.
My teeth shall have to be removed.
With pliers I jerk them out myself,
the sockets to sustain milady's pleasure.

Now toothless, I unstrap her hooks,
for she wishes me to suckle her stumps
until my gums are raw and the salty mix
of bloodied tissues fills my mouth.

We drink a symbiotic toast to celebrate
our perfect union, this splendid rape,
for she's castrated me and then herself.
I amputate her toes with care
to leave new nipples for arousal.

CONJURING REGRETS
by Eva V. Roslin

I am a demon conjured
Joyful, exuberant,
Dark heart beating with life
Absorbing tender ministrations
Now banished to emptiness again.
My summoner is full of regrets,
sorry to have called forth such a needful beast
Fading, claws digging into dirt, desperate
I return to the Underworld from which I came

WHEN YOU
by Miriam H. Harrison

i.
when you turn yourself
inside out like that
I don't know how
to hold you

when everything is raw
and bleeding, your
heart hanging low
from your chest, your
lungs quivering with
shudders, sighs
there is no safe place
to rest my hand, no way
to draw you close

when you turn yourself
inside out like that
I only want
to hold you if
I only knew
how

ii.
when you hide yourself
away like that
I don't know how
to reach you

when everything
is cold and hard, your
softest, tender self drawn
into your shell, your
motions and emotions hidden
deep in shadows
there is no window
to see you, no door
to join you

when you are hard and
I am raw, I only want
to come together—tender
to tender, self to self—in
your safe and solid shell if
only you would let
me in

FINGERS OF FEATHERS
by Rie Sheridan Rose

I stand on tiptoe
on the edge of the precipice
eyes closed
to listen to the wind.

Arms outstretched
to embrace the sky—
I feel my soul
shift on its tether.

A tingle like ants
crawling on my skin
and the wind brushes
fine black feathers…

Sprouting from my arms,
covering my fingers
until they meld
into wings of midnight.

I step forward,
fall to rise again…
wings beating as I
lift toward the moon.

WOMB HEART HEAD
by Raven Isobel Plum

Womb

I don't own
This part
It has bled
And bled
It has killed
It is dark
Perilous
None survived
A tomb

Heart

Hourglass
Steady
Counting
Speeding
When in danger
You're in danger
Running out
Of time
You are out
Of time

Head

The day can be bright
One dark thought
Plunges it to the depths
Paranoia seeps in
Self-loathing returns
Self-sabotage begins
A self-made prison
Inescapable

MY BODY, MY BOOK
by Carina Bissett

I began as a footnote
in another woman's story,
a division of desires, transformed
   —a plot device.

And so, I grew up, out of truth,
tabula rasa turned to
prayer book, pages trimmed,
spine rounded, irregularities smoothed.

I don't even remember when Man
replaced Mother, binding instruments
familiar as bone
folder applied, parchment pressed

and pressed, shape hammered,
backing boards bound,
bands gilt, decorations embossed,
ownership tooled by another

until I was finally deemed complete,
stamped *Hic liber femineo corio
convestitus est*: This book bound
with the skin of a woman—

a living tome, a testament,
perfect in my imperfections,
a *memento mori*, filigreed clasp
keyed, end papers pasted firmly in place.

And then one day, left unattended,
I flexed the binding, broke the guards,
peeled and pared, sliced and sheared
away his touch, and hers

to slip away from categories and classifications,
Dewey decimals be damned.
By my own hand, I made corrections, cancels,
instructions scoured, sanded, skin reclaimed—

    a palimpsest waiting
    for my true story to begin.

I CARRY
by Maureen O'Leary

I carry on my back a bag of girls
who come alive
Because thinking of them is the breath of life.
The strings have been cut
By them and their wicked
Scissors.
I always avoid the passive voice.
Their arms and legs
Jumble together
In various stages of fit and fat
Some are drinkers while some abstain.
One goes to church.
Two or three are
Vegetarian (or were when they were alive).
Open the sack and
Smell peppermint and girl.
Or women, I should say.
(Language matters.)

THE EDGE
by Annie Neugebauer

When my lover picks up the butcher knife
I remember wild
I remember the hunt
I remember that I am a mammal that wears clothes,
runs from spiders,
sleeps in warm places out of the rain – tucked against him.

When my lover flips the loin
and slices it into fatty rings
I watch his hands
I watch the skin on his chest pulse
I watch how his eyes don't look at all how I remember,
like another animal I can communicate with,
but something new – something other.

When my lover arranges the pieces
I feel the touch
I feel a shifting of the things inside me
I feel myself sharpen with foreboding, a clenching
as I look from him to the knife on the counter –
from this stranger to the fine blade.

Underneath, aren't we all
nothing more
than so much meat?

PIECES
by Annie Neugebauer

She walks toward him, carefully studying
where his gaze falls: her hands.
Those grasping, needy things she yearns to fill.
Without a word, she snaps them off
at the wrist,
tossing the first over her shoulder
and allowing the other to tumble to the carpet
once her teeth have undone the clasp.

Seeing his calculating regard drop to her feet,
she toes out of them,
one foot holding the heel as the first slips out,
then a sharp drop as her ankle balances
to release the other, left like a shoe on a rainy day.

It is then she realizes her arms still reach for him,
fingerless in their longing.
She cracks her head from side to side,
as if popping her neck from computer-stiffness,
and her arms slough off at the shoulders.

She stumbles the rest of the way to him
on nubbed legs, but he won't be needing shins;
he likes her on her knees, anyway.
Balanced before him, she waits until
he twists her legs off one by one
and she is left gazing up at him.

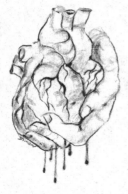

As soon as she opens her mouth
she realizes her mistake. Her words are desperate,
seeking him in soft demands
that he does not wish to hear.
She cannot argue as he plucks
the head from her neck like an errant flower.

Her eyes watch, glistening, as he squats
to push her torso back on the carpet,
as he stretches her thighs apart until they give
like strings of taffy stretched too far,
as he unzips her up the center,
and she sees her own organs, pleading
with voiceless autonomy of their own.

He forces wide the ribs, a broken bear trap,
and scoops out her pulsing heart.
The rest of her body is pushed aside even as he
sets the deep, dark muscle on the slickened carpet
and stands, looking down on it.

At least her heart's still intact,
she thinks. At least he gave her that.
She wonders what he'll do with it.

SHAMEFUL
by Lee Murray

he comes at me, my husband, her father
and I let him, too shackled by centuries
of quiet servitude. I am complicit in my demise
such is the resolve of dutiful daughters
my own leaking shameful down my legs
in a yellow sac of aborted hope and histrionics

bloodied organs on concrete leave a stain

I grasp at air for someone. Anyone. Spool
silent supplications into the darkness
with him hissing—you be quiet, woman!
I don't know how I conjure her, the tree-dwelling ghost-girl
with her whip-dark hair and razored nails
and the tell-tale spike suppurating at her throat
when she steals gruesome from the shadows. I know her
from the waft of sweetly cloying frangipani

bloodied organs on concrete leave a stain

she slits him like a grapefruit with a finger
scoops still seething between her bloodied lips
stomach and spleen seasoned in their salty sauce, she shreds
his tendons. Wreaks vengeance on the pale afterbirth
she comes at me, my sister, my mother
feckless, she devours me, too.

bloodied organs on concrete leave a stain

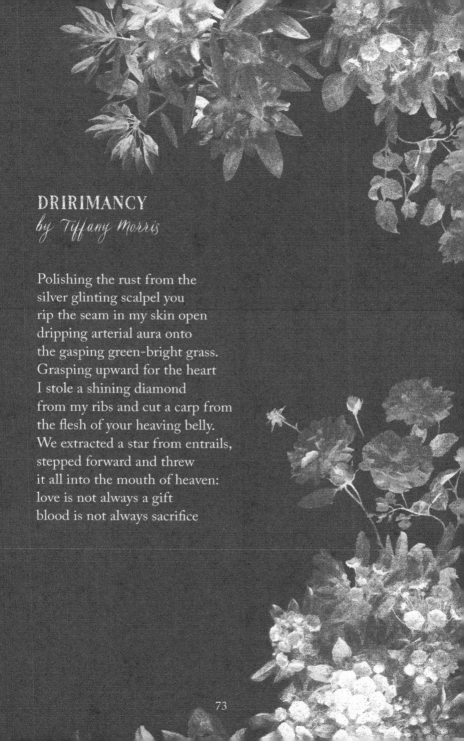

DRIRIMANCY
by Tiffany Morris

Polishing the rust from the
silver glinting scalpel you
rip the seam in my skin open
dripping arterial aura onto
the gasping green-bright grass.
Grasping upward for the heart
I stole a shining diamond
from my ribs and cut a carp from
the flesh of your heaving belly.
We extracted a star from entrails,
stepped forward and threw
it all into the mouth of heaven:
love is not always a gift
blood is not always sacrifice

EVERY MORNING
by Aimee Lowenstern

Every morning, the swallows.
Every morning I wake up, my back against the garden wall,
my chest empty. The dawn licks the grass
dew-wet. My ribs bare their teeth
and there is some scarlet trail
where my rag-tag organs bled
in the coyotes' mouths—

They were hungry. I was dead.
It was their due.

But again, the swallows.
Every morning, nestled in the curve
of my hipbone. Faces smeared with gore.
Every morning, the mud. A shallow burial,
a thousand dripping jewels. The swallows build their home
of earth and spit, the swallows build their home
in me. My eyelids split the clay,
dust falls from my lashes. It hurts.
It always hurts.
Every morning, the bleeding.
Every morning, the birdsong.

REGENERATION/COLLAPSE
by Tiffany Morris

Life blooms in strange gardens:
fig trees from stomach seeds,
a green-needled branch on a lung.

There is salve and salvation:
purple-throated toxins that
save you from the summoning void.

In the backyard there are bones
wrapped in vines, growing an eye
or a mushroom. There are fingers
dirtied with soil, scraping tar
from the sky and tearing sinew
from tissue. Listen:

there are teeth that growl praise
for rotting things and all the new
that they might bring
come spring, come hell
come collapse, come dusk,
stretching tubers, stretching petals
that wrap us in their future
regardless of whether or not
we're breathing.

LOVELY LIKE HONEY
by Brianna Malotke

She always had a mellifluous
Tone to her voice,
Like a lullaby that could put
You right at ease.

She was sweet like honey
Right down to the bone,
Her movements gentle
And her smile pleasant.

Like children drawn to the
Pink fruit of the Spindle Shrub,
They loved to gather round
And listen to stories she told.

With a cluster of children
-though none her own-
Her dulcet manner
Always put them all at ease.

One fall day, as if under a spell,
No one could leave, they were
Frozen in fear as her fairy tales
Took a frightening turn.

Soon her once bright blue eyes
Turned to dark and empty sockets,
Her soothing voice now grating
Like one long scratch on a chalkboard.

The children immobilized -terrified-

Eyes wide in terror, mouths shut,
Trembling from fear and cold
They waited for this bad dream to pass.

Her limbs, once long, elegant and smooth,
Now grey and patchy. Sores dotted her
Exposed rotting flesh, bone peeking through
The areas left bare in-between clothing.

The putrid smell overwhelmed the children,
Putting her true self on display,
Motionless they waited, praying silently
As the figure in front of them transformed.

Walking corpses weren't real was the mantra
Screaming in their heads as the lifeless figure
Ushered them closer to her, waiting
Patiently for them to follow her.

Her stitched together limbs creaked
As she led them away from their loved ones,
The ghastly sight in front of them, waiting,
The children had no way out.

Following her to the entrance of the woods
The children did not look back
For this nightmare before them
Had explained she was their mother now.

LILIES LEFT FOR MOM
by Brianna Malotke

A child needs a mother.
Someone who will watch out for them
And keep them out of danger.
Someone to nurture them
And make sure they know they're loved.

Laying here, alone in this casket,
The satin smooth and cold
Against her fading skin, the silence
Giving her plenty of time alone
To think of the endless possibilities.

She may have died and been buried
Just a few days ago,
But her bones were still strong,
Though her corpse stone cold.
She flexed her fingers,
Wiggled her toes,
Some of her flesh had started to rot
And yes, she was semi bloating
But even with the creaks of her bones
She knew it would be fine.

Partially decomposed, fully aware,
She had thought it over enough.
She knew she had to stay.
Clawing her way out
From her marked grave
She noted the lilies left
And the small notes of affection.
But she could not rest for she was
A caring mother, and after all
A child needs a mother.

GROWING PAINS
by Amy Lowenstern

Inside every young girl is an older girl,
and she is pretty & smart & thin enough
to fit between a young girl's ribs.
She lifts her mouth to the young girl's ear
and says that everything will be so perfect
when the older girl grows her skin
over the young girl, and is on the outside.
And the young girl is very tired,
so she looks forward to sleeping
curled up in her warm red intestines.

But when new skin comes, it's the wrong skin.
If the older girl is growing, then her lips are growing
from every orifice. If the older girl is growing,
then her eyelashes are growing from every pore.
Hormonal insects lay their eggsacks
in her chest. These are not the older girl's breasts.
Did the older girl have breasts? The young girl
is now older than the older girl ever was.

The young girl tries to sleep,
but there's something rotting in her lungs.
It's the older girl. She is, still,
a very beautiful corpse.

THE VOID
by Julieanne Lynch

Once upon a silent storm, a face dark and fearsome
stepped from the shore,
with outstretched arms
coming for me.
He wore a frown on downcast eyes,
and a smile that bared blades of teeth.
I hid amongst the dirt and leaves, frozen in place,
aghast with dread.
If shadows lurked beneath the skin, I fear what I see,
is what I've become.
Laboured breaths on broken sleep,
afraid of the realms of my reality.
She does not stir.
For she does not sleep.
She lingers in limbo,
where the dark matter seeps.
My unborn child knotted in weeds,
my womb, a place desolate and barren.
I cannot undo what I've begun,
recoiled in horror, all the things that I've done.
My body a temple for the hurt and the pain,
stripped bare to the core,
my blood runs free.
I am my own worst enemy,
For what I see, I hate, and love in equal unity.
My child, she dies as another lays in wait.
The things I cannot do, that a mother should do.

I hold my heart in the palm of my hands,
I beg for forgiveness; I am what I am.
My body a place where new life begins,
damaged, broken, unworthy of your kiss.
I stare in the mirror, the lines on my face,
weary and tired, unhappy; unloved
And the place you once slept,
marked with reminders of what I couldn't keep.

SPLIT
by Blaise Langlois

smile
so your lips crack and bleed
showing me
what I already know
that your beauty
is forced
and can no longer
bear witness
to your falsehood
your pride
consuming you from the inside
like decaying creatures
rotting
upon the forest floor
bones giving
under the pressure of time
speaking
in whispers of dust
to that which would devour them
that to which you
are forever
a slave

SKIN CHANGER
by Blaise Langlois

rumors
breeding in hot, whispered breath
are claims
which can no longer
be substantiated
yet, here
they are Testament
written deep in the grooves
of this covering
mapping the course
which I have taken
but somehow
lost in translation
a burden lies heavy
with pressure enough to
split
me
at
the
seams
tearing wide
exposing bone and sinew
shedding a husk
leaving myself
upon the floor
I emerge
glistening and naked
reborn

CONCEPTION
by EV Knight

Quiescent, peaceful.
Potential within woman
Within woman.
Until, in an eruption of crimson, she is evicted
It is her turn.
Hers—as soon as she
Lies still and let the seeds poke and prod until at last
(Don't fight it)
One forces itself inside
Leaving her with a new identity
Because she alone is not enough
She needs He to become
"A real woman"—XX
XX, like the dead eyes of her ancestors
Whose spilled blood wove a tapestry
All women carry within their own tumbling concavities
Blood for not bearing sons (not my fault, not my fault)
Blood for thinking differently (witch, witch! She's a witch)
Blood for making a choice (Whore! Murderer!)
XX is a death sentence
And now it is hers to serve
She kicks and squirms inside her prison cell
Her mother sighs wanly
For once, the blood doesn't come

BROKEN FINGERS
by Emma Kathryn

The First man to hold my hand
Held it tighter than any man should.
He crushed my delicate fingers with ease,
Like a rabid wolf chewing on a baby mouse.

Loosing myself from his grip was a struggle
Of shattered knuckles, ripped nails, cracked wrists.
He wasn't one for letting go of things.
Breaking free of him was worth the blood loss.

The Second man to hold my hand
Was incredibly reluctant to do so.
He looked at my injuries and blemishes
But never really looked at me.

Trust grew and I offered him my hand –
My ugly broken fingers reaching out like snapped twigs –
He touched me only when he had to.
Eventually, he admitted his repulsion, and ran.

The Third man to hold my hand
Only did so briefly.
He looked at my knuckles and palms as the first one did
And I left before he had the chance to crack them.

The Fourth man to hold my hand
Has been aware of my scars since day one.
He listens when I tell him their stories
And offers bandage and salve – if I want to take them.

There is a ring on one of my fingers now
Hiding only some of the wounds.
I am scared that if one day it slips off
My mangled ruined digit will fall off with it.

A HOME TO THOSE WHO FLY
by Naching T. Kassa

I wake to the chill of frost,
An April morning beneath,
The rich brown earth,
Slivers of wood in my pale skin.

The sun rises slowly,
Heating the world inch by inch,
Reaching into my broken casket,
Warming my companions.

The larvae have grown.
Behind my breastbone,
Their wings quiver within,
Supplanting my shriveled heart.

Pallid worms wriggle,
Through the sludge of blood,
A whisper of life,
Flowing through my veins.

The chrysalis in my throat,
Shivers against my uvula,
Crackling and peeling,
The creature emerges.

Atrophied muscle,
Fueled by thought alone,
Pushes my skeletal arms up,
Through the dirt and rock.

The world is a mystery,
The witch queen has stitched shut,
The empty windows to my soul.
Slowly, I rise from the earth.

I lift my head to the sky,
And from between my lips,
The moth crawls.
It takes flight.

SHED
by Vivian Kasley

Each month I shed.
Skin, thick layers of arid lining, painful blobs of disappointed
blood, and another chance.
Each year I shed.
Youth, tears that sting, dewy charm and tethered dreams,
friends, more blood, and more chances.
Each day I shed.
Unsolicited assurances, an armor of invulnerability,
and a moral imperative.
Each hour I shed.
Smiles that aren't intended because others know
my body better than I do.
Each of these sheds have morphed me into something else.
Something hideous and gross. A gluttonous hostile in-between.
I'm a selfish beast who'll have their cake and eat it too,
shedding just for fun, until my joyless insides wither and crack
like lines on a desert floor.
It's only then that the torches and pitchforks will be lowered,
and I'll no longer be the beast. I'll be pitied and unremarkable.
An outwardly vessel that never was but could've been.
And the last thing I will ever shed will be the soul from my
pruney carcass as it is charred into ash and bits of bone that
someone loved so freely. And that will be all that
ever really mattered.

DANSE DE LA MORT
by R. J. Joseph

Effluvia dances,
hanging in the air,
collapsing atop
the decay that composed it.
We flowed this same dual way
you and I, in love
entwined together
molded as one. Fused souls cried
out in stark unison
when the blood did flow,
seeping into the grass
we fed with disquiet. Rot.
Ecstasy turned hate
fueled our pas de deaux,
the final curtain call
for an ill-fated showing.
You took your bow first,
finality granted,
eyes open to silent
applause from a lone guest
who struggled to succumb next.
And yet, I wait still,
flies gorging on bloat,
seeking orifices
no longer dancing with life.

BETRAYER
by R.J. Joseph

No hold could take
to sustain the life within;
cold, clammy clots
clambered through,
falling as heavily as the tears.
Inviting pain,
stabbing slices synching
with pounding beats
of a broken heart.
Break the vessel;
cut jagged entrances
into the betrayer,
spraying sluice, splaying
open to invite new life
from the retrieved
losses;
losing the one hold
tenuously clinging to
living, lying lifeless
with the visionary
sensing soothing solitude
beyond the betrayal.

RELIGION FOR WOMEN
by Patricia Gomes

Reverently, I glue narrow newspaper
columns to my body —
nude and painted red. Red
for my sisters. We are all red
under the skin.
Childbirth, menstruation, united
in red.
Themed clippings these: politics, racism,
gun violence, and ads selling hope in capsule form.
Later, after I'm satisfied there no bare spots,
no blanks for the viewers to fill in
with their own imaginations,
I'll seal myself with polyurethane. Locking
it all in for eternity.
They tell me this is how it's done. The proper way.

I'm still searching for more.

Grainy pictures of women drowning.
Photos of these victims are readily available, but rare
is the image of one in the act *of*.
The ones that I've found show similar expressions:
horror, panic, desperation. I search for resignation.
Arms raised, their hair is plastered across their foreheads,
their screams immortalized.
Stop it, I try to tell them. *Go with it!*

I died this way once before.
Water filled my mouth, my eyes. My lungs squeezed
shut, but rather than fight, I forced
the hairy hands of Rescue from my thoughts
and was reborn.

WAVE BREAKER
by Vanessa Jae

Steel is wrapped around her throat,
too tight to let out the charged waves
that flow through the gaps in her ribcage.

Her ribcage used to burn in rage
before it was replaced with wires,
its metal corroding, bleeding rust.

Rust contaminates the water drowning her,
seeping through the hole in her mouth
and the crevices between her limbs.

I BEGIN TO BECOME NUMINOUS
by Juleigh Howard-Hobson

Rigor mortis sets in, then breaks down. Lack
of oxygen and sustenance causes
cells to stop renewing. Gut flora start
out of control proliferation, slack
spaces fill up with pressurized gases
and my corpse will burp, and my corpse will fart

before I bloat. In lieu of oxygen,
sulphur will mix with my hemoglobin

giving my body some nasty greenish
black spots. Swelling continues and my eyes
pop out of their sockets, rotten liquids
and putrefied organs begin to flush
out of my openings. A stench will rise
attracting attentions of the insects

who arrive to lay eggs. Bottle flies will
come first. Coffin flies, flesh eating beetles,

their maggots, then worms, then the birds, come to
gnaw / peck / chew / my meat, my skin, my gut
that still remains, even my hair becomes
a meal. Exposed bones will be used to chew
on, for sharpening front teeth of the rat
who ate my lungs, the mouse who sampled some

of my facial tissue. What's left will lay
in place while who I was erodes away.

THE DARK COCOON
by Samantha Holland

Bloating
Floating, hunting,
They come overnight.
So wetly in their hunt.
Dewdrops, past their disguise.
Uncaring women and butterflies.
Eating the minds of other men,
constant capsules, slipring.
Creepy underworld
new world, first death.
Tethered legs in a row
wetly living.
On a dripping garden wall,
let it happen to you.
Pluck, tuck, and pull,
squish them with your toe.
Butterflies and tokens,
no memory of fuzz.
Through the green sting, they glow.

AMESTRIS
by Shira Haus

I am informed that Amestris, the wife of Xerxes, when she
had grown old, made return for her own life to the god who is
said to be beneath the earth by burying twice seven children of
Persians who were men of renown.
—Herodotus, *Histories 7.114.*

I.
When telling the children about nighttime
and all the slithering beasts it hides,
Mother becomes a different creature,
and grows fingernails to match
whatever witch we're learning about
tonight. Maybe they're little swords
to protect her hands, or maybe
she is the witch. It doesn't matter—

someone must tell us about the monsters
in the attic, to *stay away* from the backyard shed
unless we'd like our eyeballs jellied,
our intestines strung from the rafters
like streamers for a birthday party.

II.
Occasionally I wake drenched in sweat,
imagining those nails tearing through my body
and must bathe everything in warm orange light
from my bedside lamp to see my skin, myself.
I press my fingers to the side of my neck;
sweat, not blood. Smooth skin, no puncture.
The ritual reminds me of that movie I can't
get out of my head, the one where the mother
goes insane, pulls a knife from her throat
and kills her whole family in the night. My nails,
too, itch to rip something apart: my throat,
maybe hers. The midnight train rumbles by,
and my dreams skitter back under the rug.
Remind yourself you're alive, a finger on the pulse
trembling through these minutes.
Say words no one should know: *astringent, asphyxiate,*
work your way through the alphabet.

When I wake up, I will clean the house.
Scour the ground until there's nothing left to see.

III.
In my favorite bedtime story
there is a little girl with two sharp horns
and wings of smoldering embers, cursed by
her mother to be lonely, wandering
along the train tracks and listening
to stones that weep under her feet.
Night extends its spindly fingers,

runs them through my hair.
If you believe in monsters as a child,
you fight them or become them.
Before the story, she would tell me:
remember. All things go the way of flowers
withering in the front yard,
starved of light and food.
And I would listen. And I remember.

IV.
Crown me queen of the animals
that hide in the small darknesses
of the world when the moon
bares its sharp, white teeth.
Hold me so tightly I can't reach
the scissors on my bedside table.
Tell me that this red-lit sky
marks where the train slows,
that this is the part of the story
where I jump off and get gravel stuck
in my throat, stones tearing
the skin from my feet. Tell me
we've come to the ending already,
when the earth comes up
to swallow the girl,
and the mother finally
opens her eyes.

MEDUSA IN FACE AND FORM
by Cordelia Harrison

They grow like weeds.
Sprouting like ragwort with its delicate insidious poison, bending like wind wrought daisies.
Grey and unpleasant as a toad's underbelly.
I feel them constantly. As a mother feels her child squirm restlessly in the womb.
They keep growing.

I pluck them each day like fine hairs. But it makes no difference. More come.
They tear through my body like rags.
Overnight they erupt. Spewing forth from white skin like minute snakes.
My skin is gorgon like. Medusa in face and form.

The young doctor's eyes are wide as a gaping abyss when he pulls back the curtain.
He does not hide his shock well. I want to laugh his efforts are so pitiful.
The nurses tend to me with gloves and masks. They say my wounds are shocking.
Their soft compassion is worse than abhorrence. I would rather they show me revulsion.
I know the fungi has made me a monster.

At night, I claw at my ravaged skin. My deformed face.
The tumours are expanding, growing voraciously.
Parasites that have taken over my form, like maggots squirming over the rot of a day old
corpse.

I am alone in my misery. I howl like a newborn into my pillow. I am unable to take this torture. Not for much longer.

My arms are bound like Prometheus. I feel like a tortoise, flailing on its back.
They are not allowing me to pluck the moulds away. Somehow this makes the torture worse.
I have a bit planted in my mouth like a horse. I scream and I scream. Howling away like the beast I am.
Nothing can stop my tears. My grief at what I have become.

My mother sits before my bedside. Weeping with blue eyes like crushed sapphires.
She berates me. Begs. She cannot understand. She speaks like the doctors. Like the nurses.
She cannot see the grotesque fungus that grows from my body.
She says there is nothing there. I have been tearing at my skin and face for no reason.
Mother says my mind has betrayed me. I am only hurting myself.

BLOODROOT
by Amanda Kirby

It was a soft, warm rain
That washed the last of the mud
From my pale face

I could almost taste
The fiddleheads
In my mouth

The early ramps
Cool
In my fingers

Reverend Jack
In his striped hood
Judging me
From the hillside

For having lain
On the forest floor
And put bloodroot to my lips

It's all around me now
As though my blood
Pooling
Birthed it instead

I lay here still
The spring sun
Brightening my cheekbones

As I toothily smile
Trillium and saxifrage
My daughters instead

A CARNIVAL OF SUFFERING
by H. Grim

I've gone missing,
a forced kidnapping,
stealing who I once was,
and the person I'll never be.

Explosions in my fingertips,
lightning strikes flicker along my veins,
torture me over and over again.

Wrapping poisonous needles,
along each vertebra,
gouging my spine,
shattering my tailbone like glass.

Embedding an ache so deep,
it will engulf in flames throughout my body,
like a living weapon,
a darkness threatening to pull me under.

I see with dimming eyes,
silently begging for the hurt to end,
to stop the pain from becoming all that I am,
and all that I'll ever be.

Like a bell that has been rung too hard,
the vibrations never-ending,
bruising my skin,
eviscerating my soul.

No space is left untouched from the pulling,
and twisting,
and ravaging.

A sinking heaviness in my chest,
as I realize that I'm trapped,
trapped inside this half-closed casket,
a deflated bag of flesh,
blood and broken bones.

There is no cure for this disease,
only survival,
only surviving.

Only.

A RECURRING NIGHTMARE
by Abigail Gray

entering the room
where i once laid my head in youth,
style and furniture in constant rotation,
the color scheme, a scalding rose for youth,
and black for bitterness,

i find the breadcrumb trail
that led me to
a familiar discovery:

i watch as she devoured the skins
of my family, father and mother
savored for last
cousins already left for mush
as the uncle rots
and teeth are sunk into
the meaty drumstick of an aunt.

she knows i am here
turns to face me,
eyes bleached and crying
while sludge bubbles
out of her nostrils, choking her
because she can't even
stop for a second to
take a breath, instead
engorging herself on tendons and scraps

"why are you doing that?"
i ask, not bothering to question

Under Her Skin

what she had done before,
seeing the paring knife and
organs spilled across the old
stained carpet gave me enough answers,
i assumed as much anyways.

she seemed annoyed i would even question her,
"because this is all we know how to do," she said,
continuing to suck out plasma
and drench herself in the muck.

realizing she was right, i felt my knees
sink, could not control my movements as i
slivered towards the skinless bodies
of my parents and began
to feast on their sins,
in utter silence of my Other,
save for the slurping of our mouths and
the occasional clink of a knife.

TRAPPED
by Kerri-Leigh Grady

First it's a finger, suddenly locked
in place, unwilling to move, unable
to bend.
Her feet turn next, too sensitive
to hold her weight, and then too stiff
to carry her properly from bed to couch.
Her body's practice complete, its recital
successful, her skin blooms with bark
in blackening ridges,
twigs burst from her joints, her fingers
twist and gnarl and curl, her jaw freezes open,
—a hollow where moss emerges—
and she reaches up, up, seeking warmth to
soften the freezing joints, but she only finds
the ceiling, where the leaves that sprout
from gray knobs that once were knuckles
pierce through with jagged, burning edges
and tear out chunks of roof, allowing the cold
rain to pour upon her, thickening the bark,
stiffening the boughs,
trapping her inside this living coffin.

CLAM BASKETS RETURNED
by Patricia Gomes

The dream reoccurs:
raking through clotted and tangled seaweed
with my bare hands
on a winter beach
    cold, isolated, wretched.
Raking, sorting, hands claw-like and bloody,
torn to shreds that dangle and tease
starving gulls.
I dig and dig,
then pull out sparkling silver threads
of Christmas tinsel. Victorious, I hold
my treasure-filled hands up to the sky
and wail,
    wail
at a bleak, diluted sun.
The tinsel begins to gleam as it latches on
to the watery light this stingy ghost sun gives back.
Intensifying. Dazzling. I stare,
sobbing through chattering teeth until it all turns
to glass.
Wailing causes the glass to shatter;
more blue now than silver, it rains down
slicing into me, blinding me.

At last, I am silent. There is no sound,
save for the churning of the sea.

To this misery,
a vicious, triumphant wave rolls forth,
crashing against the shoreline.
It lingers
on the sand for a moment;
it caresses the seaweed,
kisses the shell of a horseshoe crab.
As it retreats, green and glacial, it pulls me along,
and drags me under.

My flesh the sacrifice that closes our tourist season.

BONE KEY
by Emma J. Gibbon

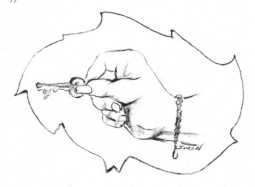

My father carved a key from bone
to fit the keyhole in my chest.
My mother breathed onto it
polished its white sheen
to ease the way
it turned in the lock
but it still caught
when I tried to turn it.
There were spurs that developed on the bit
it took time to file them all down
but it still ground in the keyway
never quite turning smoothly
the bow sticking
when pressed.
I had wanted to be a real girl
when I grew up
but
the clockwork would not shift
from dust to real.

QUEEN
by Alyson Faye

She drinks bitter bark
sups sap and slime
with a forked tongue,
slithering, she lies
swaddled in skins
red-raw, rust-stained

upon a nest of
sloughed-off dermis -
lacy cobwebs in the dirt,
whilst above
corpses of her spawn
hang mute, grisly
bunting on branches
born of myth, and misery.

Her heart's forgotten
how to mourn - only
DNA trace memories
of primeval jungles
fetid swamps
forests of Jurassic ferns
lush with the scent of death

her belly stirs

her time is nearly come.
Swollen, protruding
she splits open
roaring rage
and agony
spewing violence

this time
will be different
this time
she will not feed.

DEAR BAPTIST
by Tracy Fahey

dear baptist
with your head on a platter

do you smile?

we share a birthday
a kindred rashness
and a decolation

but I cut off my own head

(powdered my face
reddened my lips)

and served it up with a flourish

he wrinkled his nose
'no thanks salome'
he said politely
and walked away

salome?
salome?

I stood there in confusion
no, I'm the baptist
my head splashed
with a foolish look of surprise
as it dripped on the pavement

next time
next time I'll be salome
slanted smile
hand on the axe

until then

love is just one bloody surprise after the other

BETTER BY NOW
by N. J. Ember

She's circling the drain asking, "is this what we've been reduced to?"
Inner child inquires, "why is this what we are used to?"

Looming shadows, lingering phantom fingers clutch at the forefront of a forgone memory.
Too many years ahead.
She never thought there'd be an After at the edge of that The End calamity.

Drifting, the fluorescence of hospital lights remind her of summer sun.
The rays seep under lids and lie about the life to come.
Bloodied knuckled, gasping, grasping at the green grass at the precipice of undone.

This is her undoing.

Spine break, knees buckle to find a whole new shade of dark.
They will call her survival an art.
Inner child inquires, "what is life if not death at its start?"

This is her undeath.

Stop. Drawing breath for the rebirth, but part of her never rises.
Realizes, there no sequel.

There is only her and a systemic ceaseless evil. Eyes open. Re-enter the world.

Eyes open.

Sacrifice of the Final Girl.

DISSOLVING CONNECTIONS
by Stephanie Ellis

She took the bottle,
bone label warning
ignored.

Wanted to see for herself,
what ate at her
from the inside.

Felt the acid years
crawl up her throat
in bitter gratitude.

A caustic voice,
societal echo against
offending lines,
urged a cure,
a piranha solution
to her problem.

So she obliged.

With a sulphuric reduction,
layer by layer,
through flesh and blood,
she dissolved connections

and burned.

CORPSE CONSORTIUM
by Darien Dillon

shadow hand bannister reaching
for salt crusted eyelashes,
hair of sunrot seaweed,
tee-shirt moisture leeching
honeypaced puddles.

walls etched in translucence.
rubber red cubbyhole
entrusts

my liver:
grey brown
squeeze pink slimy
giggle lavishly
slop excess juice
between clavicles
slip wet on forehead
tongue bile
freckle face gall
oxidize rind luxury.

waltz heart in rapture
periphery littered:
moldering organs,
malignant glee

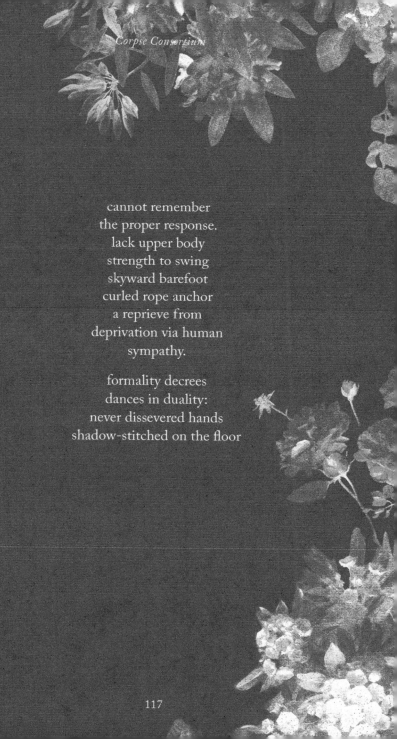

cannot remember
the proper response.
lack upper body
strength to swing
skyward barefoot
curled rope anchor
a reprieve from
deprivation via human
sympathy.

formality decrees
dances in duality:
never dissevered hands
shadow-stitched on the floor

AETOS DIOS
by Darien Dillon

Usurper, Oath-breaker, I am tasked to eat you alive.
standing, chained to the gutter gouge your eyes alive

believed faraway fantasies pressure diamonds from mud
brother's begotten luck holds earth, ground down alive

I finger your entrails, gnarled hands, nightshade nails
labor-cracked over torturing millennia I've been a live

viscera-devourer, guzzling organs before Chaos dreamt
becoming your ancestor I knew more dead than alive

creatures who roam our dried-up underbelly. Neglected
shades, riverbank's lost memorial: you call that alive?

ancient arc-swept slit throats litter our dismal shores,
grievances moan awaken latched to loathing: alive.

I, Guilt, feast on urine tinted kidneys, fresh grown liver,
while fire washed fools arrive in the Land of the Un-alive.

BITS OF YOU, STILL KEPT

by Maggie Shurtleff

I found jaw bones
Gnawing at your femur
I heard them singing
Love songs.
Pelvis full of cold air
Your hips - dusty and frail.
Eye sockets oceanless.
Sterling silver dangling still.
Could never quite catch
The flies procreating
Maggots always found their way.
Never imagined toes and fingers
The same. They are.
I can still smell pomegranate
In your hair. And thought, how lovely.
You look taller now. Laying there.
Barren. Empty. Wordless.

OUR LADY'S BIRD
by Carina Bissett

A good girl wears white
gloves, pristine, unblemished
hands folded, head bowed,
lips pressed tight, pink
heat hidden, sealed, trapped

in bleached cotton that covers,
smothers knuckles bruised,
nails chewed, cuticles torn,
blood spotting, weeping,
a testament to wickedness within.

Summer promises no salvation
sent to an Anne such as I—
transformation suffered sevenfold,
Sorrows sanctified,
Joys beheaded, annulled.

So, I stalk alleys, abandoned
lots, calling on Ladies for blessings.
And when I finally shed my skin,
reemerge, red-cloaked, elytra armored,
I will be Wild, a goddess of storms,

a supplicant no longer.
I will unfold those origami wings,
fly far away from penitence,
prayer books, accusations,
promises of perdition and hellfire.

And the bounty will be mine
to bequeath, to bless
luck gracing a good girl in white
counting spots, whispering wishes,
seeking to become something more.

THE LAST WOMAN
by Tiffany Michelle Brown

I want to feel all of you,
He says,
And his voice is an oil slick,
Intent on staining my skin
With blood and bad intentions.

I smile, knowing he's about to get much more than he paid for,
And then I oblige,
Allowing cotton, then silk, then bone
To fall to the floor.
He tries to run, except
There's nowhere to go but
Down, down, down.

He stares into my throat as I approach,
And the pink folds invite him in,
Head, shoulders, knees, and toes.
He tastes of skinned knees,
Uncauterized wounds,
Protests muffled by hotel pillows.

My esophagus welcomes him into its slippery embrace,
And I can feel him scream as peristalsis kicks in.
Contract, relax.
Contract, relax.

My body purrs when he's fully submerged and
Gastric juices break him down
Churning and burning until he's mine,
Nothing more than chyme.

I absorb his rage, his power, his sadness,
All the things he used to employ
To unwillingly pin
Others beneath him.
I convulse and contort,
Taking him in,
Swallowing his poison.

Afterward, I lay on the hotel mattress,
Trembling, coming down from the high,
Naked and smoking and soaked in sweat.

I think of the shoes I'll buy
With the crumpled-up cash on the nightstand,
Blood money turned beautiful,
And lick my lips.

When I'm finally sated and still,
I smile, imagining him
And the way he looked
When he realized I was the last woman
He'd ever fuck
With.

THE CARRION FLOWERS
by Morgan Sylvia

You had lofty dreams, didn't you, darling?
Back in those golden days before sun turned to rain
I still have photographs of that chrysalis time
The man before the monster, framed against a stormy sky
Do you know what those colors mean to me now?
Blue and purple, black and grey
Impacts that made my ears ring
Bruises blooming like flowers on my skin
My muscles constrict when I remember
Our pretty flesh is so weak, isn't it?
So vulnerable to claws and fists and teeth
Your strength lies in muscles and the history behind them
Mine is in the rage of being trapped
I will not measure my worth in hours or dollars
But in scars and breaths and missing teeth
Grace won through grit and rust and carrion severance
Hit me again (watch me shine)
Hit me again (watch me rise)
You always thought yourself a god
But in the end, we are all organs and slime
I found a way out, past the screaming, the broken glass
The blood on bathroom walls
That chic dark tile that never showed your sins
You brought me into the cellar so nobody heard my screams
Cement echoes sound in a way singers envy
Sometimes I focused on the reverb
My rage was wet and bloody
My rage smelled of death
Memories strike like your blows

I recall your voice twisting on smoke
Raise you another grand
Kings and queens stare out from grimy cards
Do another shot, darling. Hit me again
They can put me in chains, turn your lies into charges as they
did once before
Words on paper versus blood on the floor
My left eye is useless now, and my pinky won't bend
I only understood when the scars healed into armor
I could never escape you
Because I was always free
I put your eyes in a silver box
Keep it by my bed so you can still watch me sleep
Your heart I put in a jar of rocks
I tossed it into the sea with the other foul slimy things
Waters cold and dark as your soul
Your feet and fists are buried beneath the apple tree
With the child that never breathed
Your tongue I gave to the lilacs
The rest of you is in the rose garden
Our love
has finally grown into something beautiful

ABOUT THE EDITORS

Lindy Ryan is an entrepreneur, award-winning analytics professor, and publishing professional. In 2017, Ryan founded Black Spot Books, an independent small press focused in speculative fiction, which was acquired by Vesuvian Media Group in 2019. Ryan currently serves on the Board of Directors for the Independent Book Publishers Association (IBPA) and, in 2020, was named one of *Publishers Weekly*'s Star Watch Honorees.

Ryan is a multi-genre award-winning and bestselling editor and author with a catalog spread from non-fiction to horror, historical fantasy, and contemporary romance. Her books have received numerous awards, and several have been adapted for screen. Currently, she is collaborating as the lead author on a horror franchise project with a top veteran Hollywood director and an award-winning screenwriter.

When she's not immersed in books, Ryan is an avid historical researcher, with specific interest in nautical and maritime history, cryptozoology, and ancient civilizations. She is represented by Gandolfo Helin & Fountain Literary Management, supported by Meryl Moss Media, and is an active member of numerous literary organizations, including the Horror Writers Association and the Romance Writers of America. Lindy can be found online at www. glitterandgravedust.com or on social media @LindyRyanWrites.

Toni Miller is a twenty-year veteran in technology, where she leads software development and releases for a multinational tech company. She is a long-time fixture in the horror literary community, where she works to actively champion underrepresented voices in the genre. Miller is a co-founder of the Ladies of Horror Fiction and the host of the Ladies of Horror Fiction Podcast. She also reviews horror and dark fiction and has authored several non-fiction pieces in *Aphotic Realm Magazine*. Find Toni online at www.themisadventuresofareader.com or on Twitter @Toni_The_Reader.

ABOUT THE POETS

Desiree Abalos is a Mexican American writer and grad student who specializes in the darker themes of poetry and short fiction. She currently lives in Ontario, CA. Her previous work can be found in *The Rush Magazine LA* and her other works can be found on her blog at https://lewilddesi.com.

Nico Bell is the author of *Food Fright* and the editor of *Shiver*. She has several short stories published in a variety of outlets including the *Gothic Blue Book VI: A Krampus Carol* and *The Second Corona Book of Horror Stories*. She can be found online at www.nicobellfiction.com and on Twitter and Instagram @ nicobellfiction.

Carina Bissett is a writer, poet, and educator working primarily in the fields of dark fiction and fabulism. Her short fiction and poetry have been published in multiple journals and anthologies including *Upon a Twice Time, Bitter Distillations: An Anthology of Poisonous Tales, Arterial Bloom, Gorgon: Stories of Emergence, Hath No Fury, and the HWA Poetry Showcase Vol. V and VI*. She is also the co-editor of *Shadow Atlas: Dark Landscapes of the Americas*. Links to her work can be found at http://carinabissett.com.

Melodie Bolt is an American poet and writer based in Flint, Michigan. She has been a member of the Flint Area Writers for over a decade and is a lifetime member of SFPA. Her fiction and poetry have been published in venues such as *Aphotic Realm, Prairie Schooner, Paper Dragon, Pussy Magic, Verse Wisconsin, TOTU, Yellow Medicine Review, Witches & Pagans*, and a blog post on *Cemetery Travel*. She earned an MFA—Writing from Pacific University, and a Master's in English from University of Michigan—Flint. She is the recipient of the James Tiptree Jr. Fairy Godmother Award and a past finalist for the Speculative

Literature Foundation's Working Writers Grant. You can find her on Twitter @Melodie_Bolt, on Goodreads, Facebook, and https://www.melodiebolt.com/.

Nancy Brewka-Clark is a member of the New England Horror Writers and the Short Mystery Fiction Society. Brewka-Clark has been honored to have her work in *Yellow Mama*, *Close to the Bone*, *Eastern Iowa Review*, *Litbreak*, *Every Day Fiction*, *Twist in Time*, *The First Line*, two anthologies of drabbles by Australian publishers Black Hare Press and Bloodsong Books, five collections of Gothic horror published by FunDead Publications of Salem, and the original pizza horror anthology *Tales from the Crust*. Kelsay Books published her debut poetry collection *Beautiful Corpus* in March 2020.

Tiffany Michelle Brown is a California-based writer who once had a conversation with a ghost over a pumpkin beer. Her fiction has been featured by Sliced Up Press, Cemetery Gates Media, Fright Girl Summer, and the NoSleep Podcast. Tiffany lives near the beach with her husband, Bryan, their pups, Biscuit and Zen, and their combined collections of books, board games, and general geekery.

Elsa M. Carruthers is a poet and writer whose poems have published in *Space and Time Magazine*, *Nonbinary Review*, *Uppagus*, and the *HWA Poetry Showcase*.

Linda M. Crate is a Pennsylvanian writer. Her poetry, short stories, articles, and reviews have been published in a myriad of magazines both online and in print. She has seven published chapbooks: *A Mermaid Crashing Into Dawn* (Fowlpox Press, June 2013), *Less Than A Man* (The Camel Saloon, January 2014), *If Tomorrow Never Comes* (Scars Publications, August 2016), *My Wings Were Made to Fly* (Flutter Press, September 2017), *Splintered with Terror* (Scars Publications, January 2018), *More Than Bone Music* (Clare Songbirds Publishing House, March

2019), and *The Samurai* (Yellow Arrowing Publishing, October 2020), and two micro-chapbooks, *Heaven Instead* (Origami Poems Project, May 2018) and *Moon Mother* (Origami Poems Project, March 2020). She is also the author of the novel *Phoenix Tears* (Czykmate Books, June 2018). She also has three full-length poetry collections, the latest being *Mythology of My Bones* (Cyberwit, August 2020).

Shy and nocturnal, **Jennifer Crow** has rarely been photographed in the wild, but it's rumored that she lives near a waterfall in western New York. You can find other examples of her poetry on several websites and in various print magazines including *Uncanny Magazine*, *Kaleidotrope*, and *Analog Science Fiction*. She's always happy to connect with readers on her Facebook author page or on Twitter @writerjencrow.

Darien Dillon often stays up too late indulging in all-things horror, which probably explains the bizarre and gruesome dreams she uses to fuel her works. Darien's macabre poetry is featured in *The Scribe Magazine*, *The Literary Hatchet*, and *Penumbric Speculative Fiction Magazine*. You can find her on Twitter @Darien_Dillon.

Stephanie Ellis writes dark speculative prose and poetry and has been published in a variety of magazines and anthologies. Her latest work includes the novel, *The Five Turns of the Wheel* and the novella, *Bottled*, both published by Silver Shamrock. She has been published in Flame Tree Press' *A Dying Planet* anthology, the charity anthology *Diabolica Britannica*, and is included in Silver Shamrock's *Midnight in the Pentagram* anthology. She is co-editor of *Trembling with Fear*, HorrorTree.com's online magazine. She is an affiliate member of the HWA and can be found at https://stephanieellis.org and on Twitter at @el_stevie.

N. J. Ember is a paranormal fiction author who loves to write stories about survival and triumph over adversity. Whether

her characters are dealing with the paranormal or everyday life, she seeks to show that strength is not always about being superhuman or invulnerable. She enjoys anything with mystery, suspense and horror, so when she's not writing you can find her watching shows like Orphan Black, Penny Dreadful, and Sherlock. She currently lives in Michigan with her grandpa and a forever growing collection of books and Funko Pop! figures.

Marilyn Fabiola is a Brooklyn based Guatemalan writer, a ravenous reader, and a lover of the dark and horrific. She holds a Bachelor of Arts in History from St. John's University and is currently the Assistant Editor of Maximalist Press, an imprint devoted to showcasing POC and Queer literature.

Tracy Fahey is an Irish writer. She has written a PhD on the Gothic, and published one novel and three collections on domestic unease, folk horror, and most recently on body horror (*I Spit Myself Out*, Sinister Horror Company, 2021). She also writes poetry and has had work published in US-based journal *High Shelf*.

Alyson Faye lives in West Yorkshire, UK, with her husband, teen son, and rescue animals. Her fiction and poetry has been published in a range of anthologies, (e.g. *Diabolica Britannica/ Daughters of Darkness*) on the Horror Tree site, several *Siren's Call*, on *Page and Spine*, by Demain Press (The Lost Girl/Night of the Rider), in *Trickster's Treats 4* and the *Sylvia* ezine. She has work due out later in 2021with Kandisha Press, Space and Time, July edition and Brigid's Gate Press' Were-Tales anthology. Alyson's work has been read on BBC Radio, local radio, on several podcasts (Ladies of Horror and The Night's End), and her poem 'Feathertide' was recently placed in the ten finalists of the Crystal Lake poetry competition. She swims, sings in a choir, and is often to be found roaming the moor with her Labrador cross, Roxy, madly throwing sticks and balls. On Twitter @AlysonFaye2.

Emma J. Gibbon is a Rhysling-nominated speculative poet and horror writer who lives in the woods in Maine. Her poetry has been published in *Strange Horizons*, *Kaleidotrope*, *Liminality*, *Eye to the Telescope*, and *Pedestal Magazine*. Her debut fiction collection, *Dark Blood Comes from the Feet*, was an NPR 2020 book of the year and won the Maine Literary Book Award for Speculative Fiction.

Currently in her second term as Poet Laureate of New Bedford, Massachusetts, author and playwright **Patricia Gomes** and has been published in numerous literary journals and anthologies. A 2018 and 2008 Pushcart Prize nominee, Ms. Gomes recent publications include *Star*Line*, *Muddy River Review*, *Rituals*, *Alien Buddha Press*, and *Apex and Abyss*.

Kerri-Leigh Grady is a software developer, terrible archer, lover of ghost investigation shows with lots of screaming and running, awful metalsmith, burgeoning woodturner, hobby collector, and obsessive list maker. You can find her wasting time on Twitter at @klgrady_ and klgrady.com.

Abigail Gray is an incoming Masters of Publishing & Writing candidate at Emerson College who currently slinks through the marshes near their childhood home in New Hampshire. Most of their writing centers around nature, gender, sobriety/addiction and mental health. They have been previously been published in *Willard & Maple*, Champlain College's *The Well*, and *Poet's Choice*. Currently, they are nurturing their first poetry manuscript, which hopes to find a home soon, as well as championing their writing and wellness blog, the dearies project.

Amy Grech has sold over 100 stories to various anthologies and magazines including: *A New York State of Fright*, *Apex Magazine*, *Dead Harvest*, *Flashes of Hope*, *Gorefest*, *Hell's Heart*, *Hell's Highway*, *Hell's Mall*, *Needle Magazine*, *Punk Noir Magazine*, *Scare You To Sleep*, *Tales from the Canyons of the Damned*, *Tales* *from The Lake Vol. 3, The One That Got Away, Thriller Magazine,* and many others. She is an Active Member of the Horror Writers Association and the International Thriller Writers who lives in New York. You can connect with Amy on Twitter @amy_grech or visit her website https://www.crimsonscreams.com.

H. Grim is a queer, chronically ill freelance writer living in Canada with a house full of wild creatures, two of which were cut from her insides. When not writing, she's probably adventuring in a moody forest somewhere. You can find her enthusiastically yelling about books on social media as The GrimDragon.

Cordelia Harrison has a fascination for all things gothic and macabre. She primarily writes dark fiction. Her stories have appeared in *Raven Review, Aphotic Realm, Mirror Dance* and *Idle Ink.* You can find her on Twitter @atsumistress.

Miriam H. Harrison studies full time, works on the side, writes when she should be doing other things, and trains the dust bunnies to fend for themselves. She is an Active member of the Horror Writers Association, and her writings can be found dismembered and scattered in various dark corners.

Shira Haus is a poet from Michigan and an English student at Allegheny College who loves horror stories. Her work has been featured in publications that include *Capsule Stories Magazine, The Albion Review,* and *Coffin Bell Journal.* You can find her on Twitter at @shira_leah.

Samantha Holland is a wife, mother of three, full-time student, and an aspiring poet. She spends most of her free time exploring the Greater Zion area in all its glory. She credits such writers for her inspiration to include Charlotte Smith, Mary Oliver, Nicolette Sowder, Stevie Smith, and Margaret Atwood. She is especially captivated by Virginia Woolf's quote, "All extremes of feeling are allied with madness." Through her writing, she hopes to capture a small glimpse of thought-provoked madness in which she calls poetry.

Juleigh Howard-Hobson's work has appeared in many places, including *Think Journal*, *Able Muse*, *Mezzo Cammin*, *Third Wednesday*, *Verse Wisconsin*, *Valparaiso Poetry Review*, *Consequence*, and *The Lyric*. She is a Million Writers "Notable Writer," has won the ANZAC Award, and has been nominated for the Pushcart, the Best of the Net, the Rhysling, and the Elgin.

Vanessa Jae writes speculative poems and short stories. She volunteers as slush reader for *Apex Magazine* and translator for *Progressive International*. Jae also collects black hoodies and bruises in mosh pits on Tuesday nights. To read tweets by interesting people, follow her at @thevanessajae.

R. J. Joseph earned her MFA in Writing Popular Fiction from Seton Hill University and currently works as an associate professor of English in Houston, TX. She has had several stories published in various venues, including two anthologies of horror written by Black, female writers, the Bram Stoker Award® finalist *Sycorax's Daughters and Black Magic Women*, as well as in *Paranormal Contact: A Quiet Horror Confessional*, and the Halloween 2020 issue of *Southwest Review*. Her academic essays have also appeared in applauded collections, such as the Bram Stoker Award® finalists "Uncovering Stranger Things: Essays on Eighties Nostalgia, Cynicism and Innocence in the Series" and "The Streaming of Hill House: Essays on the Haunting Netflix Series". Her essay from The Streaming of Hill House, "The Beloved Haunting of Hill House: An Examination of Monstrous Motherhood", was also a Bram Stoker Award® finalist for 2020.

Vivian Kasley hails from the land of the strange and unusual: Florida. She's a writer of short stories and poetry which have appeared in various science fiction anthologies, horror anthologies, horror magazines, and webzines. Some of her street cred includes Blood Bound Books, Dark Moon Digest, Gypsum Sound Tales, Ghost Orchid Press, Castrum Press, Hellbound Books, Sirens Call Publications, and most recently The Denver Horror Collective. She's got more in the works, including an upcoming tale in *Vastarien* and her very first novella. When not writing or subbing at the local middle school, she spends her time reading in bubble baths, snuggling her rescue cats and dogs, going on foodie dates with her other half, and searching for seashells and other treasures along the beach. On Twitter at @VKasley.

Naching T. Kassa is a member of the Horror Writers Association. She has over thirty short stories published (the most recent is the short story, "The Case of the Broken Needle," which appears in *The Meeting of the Minds: Sherlock Holmes and Solar Pons 1*, published by Belanger Books). She lives in Eastern Washington State with her husband, Dan, their three children, and their dogs. Naching also serves as an interviewer and Head of Publishing for Horroraddicts.net. She works as an assistant and staff writer for Still Water Bay at Crystal Lake Publishing.

Emma Kathryn is a horror fanatic from Glasgow, Scotland. You can find her on Twitter @girlofgotham. When she's not scaring herself to death, she is either podcasting as one half of The Yearbook Committee Podcast or streaming indie games on Twitch.

Lindsay King-Miller is the author of *Ask a Queer Chick: A Guide to Sex, Love, and Life for Girls who Dig Girls* (Plume, 2016). Her fiction has appeared in the anthologies *The Fiends in the Furrows* (Nosetouch, 2018), *Terror at 5280'* (Denver Horror Collective, 2019), *Tiny Nightmares* (Catapult, 2020), and numerous other publications. She lives in Denver, CO.

Amanda Kirby, introverted nature enthusiast, hails from rural Ontario. A hobby-farming homemaker, for the time being, she ekes out moments for back-country camping, kayaking the local waterways, spinning and weaving fiber, as well as writing poetry and narrative fiction. She aspires to become a full-time student in an assortment of fields including biology, anthropology, and the arts. She once caught a ground hog with her bare hands and lived to regret it.

EV Knight is a Bram Stoker Award® Winning author of horror and dark fiction. Her debut novel, *The Fourth Whore*, was released in early 2020 by Raw Dog Screaming Press. She also released the novella *Dead Eyes* in 2020 as part of Unnerving's Rewind or Die series. EV's short stories can be found in *Siren's Call* magazine and the anthologies *Monstrous Feminine* from Scary Dairy Press, *The Toilet Zone* from Hellbound Books, *More Lore from the Mythos* and its second volume from Fractured Mind Publishing, and a poem in the *HWA 2019 Poetry Showcase* titled "Nothing." A graduate of Seton Hill University, she received her MFA in Writing Popular Fiction in January 2019. She enjoys all things macabre, whether they be film, TV, podcast, novel, or short story. She lives in one of the countries most haunted cities— Savannah, GA—with her family and three crazy hairless cats.

Blaise Langlois will never turn down the chance to tell a creepy story around the campfire. After a long struggle with her inner critic, she made the decision to write down her tales in between teaching and raising four beautiful children. You are sure to find her feverishly scratching out ideas (which to the chagrin of her supportive husband, usually occurs just after midnight). She has a penchant for horror, sci-fi, fantasy and dystopia. Recently, she has renewed her love of speculative poetry. Her current and upcoming publications are through Eerie River Publishing, *Pulp Factory E-zine*, Black Hare Press, *Space and Time Magazine*, Black Spot Books, and Ghost Orchid Press. You can learn more about Blaise's writing journey by visiting her blog at www.ravenfictionca.wordpress.com.

Nikki R. Leigh is a forever-90s-kid wallowing in all-things horror. When not writing horror fiction and poetry, she can be found creating custom horror-inspired toys, making comics, and hunting vintage paperbacks. She reads her stories to her partner and her cat, one of which gets scared very easily.

Aimee Lowenstern is a twenty-two-year-old poet living in Nevada. She has cerebral palsy and is fond of glitter.

Donna Lynch is a horror and dark fiction author, a two-time Bram Stoker Award®-nominated poet, and musician from Maryland. Her work often combines elements of body horror, psychological horror, trauma, and folklore.

Julieanne Lynch is a Dragon Award-nominated author of YA and adult genre books, specializing in horror, fantasy and contemporary women's fiction. Julieanne was born in Northern Ireland, but spent much of her early life in London until her family relocated back to NI in the early nineties. Julieanne lives in Northern Ireland with her family, where she is a full-time author. She studied English Literature and Creative Writing at The Open University. Julieanne is represented by Italia Gandolfo and Gandolfo Helin & Fountain Literary Management and has several projects optioned for film.

Brianna Malotke is a freelance writer and member of the Horror Writers Association. Some of her most recent work can be found online at *The Yard: Crime Blog*, in the digital magazine *The Crypt*, and in the August 2021 issue of *Witch House Amateur Magazine*. She has poems in the hundred-word horror anthologies, *Beneath*, *Cosmos*, and *The Deep*. She is a Writer-in-Residence at the Chateau Orquevaux in Orquevaux, France in 2022.

Caitlin Marceau is an author and lecturer living and working in Montreal. She holds a B.A. in Creative Writing, is a member of both the Horror Writers Association and the

Quebec Writers' Federation, and spends most of her time writing horror and experimental fiction. She's been published for journalism, poetry, as well as creative non-fiction, and has spoken about horror literature at several Canadian conventions. Her collections, *Palimpsest* and *A Blackness Absolute*, are slated for publication by Ghost Orchid Press and D&T Publishing LLC in 2022. If she's not covered in ink or wading through stacks of paper, you can find her ranting about issues in pop culture or nerding out over a good book. For more, check out CaitlinMarceau.ca.

Jessica McHugh is a novelist, poet, and internationally produced playwright running amok in the fields of horror, sci-fi, young adult, and wherever else her peculiar mind leads. She's had twenty-four books published in twelve years, including her bizarro romp *The Green Kangaroos*, her YA series "The Darla Decker Diaries," and her Bram Stoker Award®-nominated blackout poetry collection *A Complex Accident of Life*. For more info about publications and blackout poetry commissions, please visit McHughniverse.com.

Tiffany Meuret is a writer of monsters and angry women. Her short fiction and poetry can be found in multiple online formats and magazines, and her debut novel, *A Flood of Posies*, released in February 2021 from Black Spot Books. Her upcoming novella *Little Bird* will be released in 2022. Tiffany lives in Phoenix with her husband and children. Find her online at TiffanyMeuret.com.

Tiffany Morris is a Mi'kmaw/settler writer of speculative poetry and fiction from Kjipuktuk (Halifax), Nova Scotia. She is the author of the Elgin-nominated chapbook *Havoc in Silence* (Molten Molecular Minutiae, 2019). Her work has appeared in *Uncanny Magazine*, *Abyss & Apex*, and *Vastarien*, among others. Find her online at tiffmorris.com or on Twitter @tiffmorris.

Lee Murray is a multi-award-winning author-editor from Aotearoa-New Zealand (*Sir Julius Vogel, Australian Shadows*) and a double Bram Stoker Award®-winner. A NZSA Honorary Literary Fellow, she is the Grimshaw Sargeson Fellow for 2021 for her narrative poetry collection *Fox Spirit on a Distant Cloud*. Read more at leemurray.info

Annie Neugebauer is a two-time Bram Stoker Award®-nominated author with work appearing and forthcoming in more than a hundred publications, such as Cemetery Dance, Apex, Black Static, and *Year's Best Hardcore Horror Volumes 3, 4*, and *5*. She is an Active member of the Horror Writers Association and a columnist and instructor for the *Writer's Digest* award-winning website LitReactor. Annie is represented by Alec Shane of Writers House.

Betsy Nicchetta loves collecting, reading, and reviewing horror novels. She writes book reviews and essays about bookish things on her blog www.glamorousbookgal.blogspot.com. She shares a passion for decorating her apartment in St. Paul, MN with macabre things with her husband. She also loves listening to opera and watching dogs walk their people.

Cindy O'Quinn is an Appalachian writer who grew up in the mountains of West Virginia. In 2016, Cindy and her family moved to the northern woods of Maine, where she continues to write horror stories and speculative poetry. Her work has been published or is forthcoming in *Shotgun Honey Presents Vol 4: RECOIL, The Twisted Book of Shadows Anthology, Shelved: Appalachian Resilience During Covid-19 Anthology, HWA Poetry Showcase Vol. V, Space & Time Magazine, Nothing's Sacred Vol. 4 & 5, Sanitarium Magazine*, and others. Cindy is a multiple Rhysling Award nominated poet, Dwarf Star nominee, and two-time Bram Stoker Award® nominee. You can follow Cindy for updates on Facebook @CindyOQuinnWriter, Instagram @ cindy.oquinn, and Twitter @COQuinnWrites.

Cynthia "Cina" Pelayo is a two-time Bram Stoker Awards®-nominated poet and author. She is the author of *Loteria, Santa Muerte, The Missing,* and *Poems of My Night,* all of which have been nominated for International Latino Book Awards. *Poems of My Night* was also nominated for an Elgin Award. Her recent collection of poetry, *Into the Forest and All the Way Through* explores the epidemic of missing and murdered women in the United States. Her modern-day horror retelling of the Pied Piper fairy tale, *Children of Chicago* was released by Agora / Polis Books in 2021. She holds a Bachelor of Arts in Journalism, a Master of Science in Marketing, a Master of Fine Arts in Writing, and is a Doctoral Candidate in Business Psychology. Cina was raised in inner city Chicago, where she lives with her husband and children. Find her online at www.cinapelayo.com and on Twitter @cinapelayo.

Raven Isobel Plum writes about the things that go bump in the night. She's afraid of the dark, but admits that "Not good enough" is more terrifying than any demon. Raven's works live to be thrilling on the surface and have deeper secrets for those who dare to look for them. Find her online at www.ripstories.net, or on Instagram @raven_isobelplum.

Canadian author **Mary Rajotte** has a penchant for penning nightmarish tales of folk horror and paranormal suspense. Her work has been published in *Shroud Magazine,* The Library of Horror Press, the Great Lakes Horror Company, Magnificent Cowlick Media, Fabled Collective, and Burial Day Books. Sometimes camera-elusive but always coffee-fueled, you can find Mary at her website www.maryrajotte.com or support her Patreon for exclusive fiction at www.patreon.com/maryrajotte.

Rie Sheridan Rose multitasks. A lot. Her poetry appears in numerous venues, including *Speculative Poets of Texas, Vol. 1, Texas Poetry Calendar,* and *Illumen.* She has authored six poetry chapbooks—two of which feature Horror and other Dark poetry—twelve novels, and lyrics for dozens of songs. She is an Affiliate Member of the Horror Writers Association. She tweets as @RieSheridanRose.

Eva Roslin writes dark fantasy and horror fiction. She is a recipient of the Mary Wollstonecraft Shelley Scholarship, awarded by the Horror Writers' Association. She is a Supporting HWA member. Her work has appeared in such publications as *Dark Heroes* (Pill Hill Press), *Murky Depths*, *Ghostlight Magazine*, and others.

Marge Simon is a writer/poet/illustrator living in Ocala, FL, USA. A multiple Bram Stoker Award® winner and Grand Master of SFPA, her works appear in Asimov's, Daily Science Fiction, Silver Blade, and anthologies such as *Spectral Realms*, *Chiral Mad* series, *Death by Water*, *You*, *Human*, and *Birthing Monsters*. http://margesimon.com

Monique Snyman lives in Pretoria, South Africa, with her husband, daughter, and an adorable Chihuahua. She's the author of the Bram Stoker Award®-nominated novels, *The Night Weaver* and *The Bone Carver*, and the upcoming South African horror series, *Dark Country*.

Roni Stinger lives in Vancouver, Washington. When she's not writing strange dark stories and poems, she's wandering the forests, beaches, and streets in search of shiny objects and creative sparks. Her work has been published in *Hypnos Magazine*, *Through Other Eyes by All Worlds Wayfarer*, and *HWA Poetry Showcase Volume VII*. You can find her online at www.ronistinger.com.

Dalena Storm is a graduate of the Bennington MFA program in Fiction. She has lived in Oregon, Japan, India, and Germany, before settling in the Berkshires in an old converted general store where she lives with her philosophizing husband, energetic daughter, and two feisty cats. Her most notable work to date is *The Hungry Ghost*

(Black Spot Books, 2019). You can find her online at dalenastorm.com, or occasionally on Instagram @dalenastorm.

Angela Sylvaine is a self-described cheerful goth who still believes in monsters. Her debut novella, *Chopping Spree*, an homage to 1980s slashers and mall culture, is available now. Her short fiction has appeared in multiple publications and anthologies, including *Places We Fear to Tread* and *Not All Monsters*. A North Dakota girl transplanted to Colorado, she lives with her sweetheart and three creepy cats on the front range of the Rockies. You can find her online angelasylvaine.com.

Morgan Sylvia is an Aquarius, a metalhead, coffee addict, and a work in progress. Her short fiction has appeared in several places, including *Pseudopod*, *Coming Through In Waves: Crime Fiction Inspired by Pink Floyd*, *Wicked Witches*, *Northern Frights*, *Endless Apocalypse*, *Haunted House Short Stories*, and *The Final Summons*. She is also the author of a horror novel, *Abode*; a fantasy novel, *Dawn*; and two poetry collections, *Whispers from the Apocalypse* and *As The Seas Turn Red*, which was nominated for an Elgin Award twice. Sylvia currently lives in Maine with her boyfriend, two cats, the best dog ever, and a chubby goldfish. You can keep up with her online at www.morgansylvia.com.

Sara Tantlinger is the author of the Bram Stoker Award®-winning *The Devil's Dreamland: Poetry Inspired by H.H. Holmes*, and the Bram Stoker Award®-nominated works *To Be Devoured*, *Cradleland of Parasites*, and *Not All Monsters*. Along with being a mentor for the HWA Mentorship Program, she is also a co-organizer for the HWA Pittsburgh Chapter. She embraces all things macabre and can be found lurking in graveyards or on Twitter @SaraTantlinger, at saratantlinger.com and on Instagram @inkychaotics

Stephanie Athena Valente lives in Brooklyn, NY. Her published works include *Hotel Ghost*, *waiting for the end of the*

world, *Little Fang*, and *Spell Work* (Bottlecap Press & Giallo). She has writing featured in *Witch Craft Magazine*, *Maudlin House*, and *Hobart*. She is the associate editor at *Yes, Poetry*. Sometimes, she feels human. stephanievalente.com

Emily Ruth Verona received her Bachelor of Arts in Creative Writing and Cinema Studies from The State University of New York at Purchase. Previous publication credits include work featured in *Indigo Rising*, *The Pinch*, *LampLight Magazine*, *Mystery Tribune*, and *The Ghastling*. She lives in New Jersey with a very small dog. For more visit www.emilyruthverona.com or follow her on Twitter @emilyrverona.

Antonia Rachel Ward is an author of horror, gothic and supernatural fiction based in Cambridgeshire, UK. Her short stories and flash fiction have been published by Black Hare Press and Gypsum Sound Tales, among others. She is also the founder and editor-in-chief of Ghost Orchid Press.

Cassondra Windwalker is a poet, essayist, and novelist presently writing full-time from the southern Alaskan coast. Her novels and full-length poetry collections are available online and in bookstores.

L. Marie Wood is an award-winning psychological horror author and screenwriter. She won the Golden Stake Award for her novel *The Promise Keeper*. Her screenplays have won Best Horror, Best Afrofuturism/Horror/Sci-Fi, and Best Short Screenplay awards at several film festivals. Wood's short fiction has been published widely, most recently in *Slay: Stories of the Vampire Noire* and Bram Stoker Award®-nominated anthology, *Sycorax's Daughters*. Learn more about L. Marie Wood at www.lmariewood.com or join the discussion on Twitter @LMarieWood1.

Tabatha Wood lives in Wellington, the 'Coolest Little Capital' of Aotearoa, New Zealand. She writes weird, unsettling fiction and uplifting poetry, mostly under the influence of strong coffee. A former English teacher and school library manager, her first published books were nonfiction guides aimed at professional educators. She now tutors from home, while working as a freelance writer and editor. Her debut collection *Dark Winds over Wellington* was shortlisted for a Sir Julius Vogel award in 2020, and she was shortlisted for three Australian Shadows Awards in 2021 for horror nonfiction and edited work. You can find more of Tabatha's writing and creative projects at her website tabathawood.com or on Facebook at www.facebook.com/tlwood.wordweaver/.

Stephanie M. Wytovich is an American poet, novelist, and essayist. Her work has been showcased in numerous venues such as *Weird Tales, Gutted: Beautiful Horror Stories, Fantastic Tales of Terror, Year's Best Hardcore Horror: Volume 2, The Best Horror of the Year: Volume 8*, as well as many others. Wytovich is the Poetry Editor for Raw Dog Screaming Press, an adjunct at Western Connecticut State University, Southern New Hampshire University, and Point Park University, and a mentor with Crystal Lake Publishing. She is a member of the Science Fiction Poetry Association, an Active member of the Horror Writers Association, and a graduate of Seton Hill University's MFA program for Writing Popular Fiction. Her Bram Stoker Award®-winning poetry collection, *Brothel*, earned a home with Raw Dog Screaming Press alongside *Hysteria: A Collection of Madness, Mourning Jewelry, An Exorcism of Angels, Sheet Music to My Acoustic Nightmare*, and most recently, *The Apocalyptic Mannequin*. Her debut novel, *The Eighth*, is published with Dark Regions Press. Follow Wytovich on her blog at http://stephaniewytovich.blogspot.com/ and on Twitter and Instagram @SWytovich and @thehauntedbookshelf.

Mercedes M. Yardley is a dark fantasist who wears poisonous flowers in her hair. She is the author of *Beautiful Sorrows*, the Stabby Award-winning *Apocalyptic Montessa and Nuclear Lulu: A Tale of Atomic Love*, *Pretty Little Dead Girls*, and *Nameless*. She won the Bram Stoker Award® for her story 'Little Dead Red' and is a multiple Bram Stoker Award® nominee. You can find her at mercedesmyardley.com.